A RURAL
REVOLUTION

A RURAL
REVOLUTION

THE HISTORY OF A STAFFORDSHIRE FAMILY
AND THEIR VILLAGE

DAVID R ROBERTS

Matador
9 Priory Business Park,
Wistow Road, Kibworth Beauchamp,
Leicestershire. LE8 0RX
Tel: 0116 279 2299
Email: books@troubador.co.uk
Web: www.troubador.co.uk/matador
Twitter: @matadorbooks

ISBN 978 1784625 207

British Library Cataloguing in Publication Data.
A catalogue record for this book is available from the British Library.

Printed and bound in the UK by TJ International, Padstow, Cornwall
Typeset in 12pt Aldine401 BT by Troubador Publishing Ltd, Leicester, UK

Matador is an imprint of Troubador Publishing Ltd

To Jessica Joan

Contents

Foreword

This is a story of journeys and of change. It traces one family's move from the county of Cheshire and charts their new life in a Staffordshire village. The journey is short in distance but long in duration.

At the same time, it is an exploration of some of the key changes of the world's first industrial revolution. Journeys lay at the heart of these changes as Britain's industrialisation both involved and depended upon radical developments in how people and things were moved from place to place. The country's transport network and system of communications were revolutionised by the building of canals, improvements to roads and the coming of the railways.

The story is also about the consequences of these journeys and changes. As the journeys intertwine, their impact over the decades and generations that follow is transformational – for the family, for the village and for the wider society.

Although the term 'industrial revolution' was not in general use in Britain until the late 1800s, the process to which it refers started in the previous century. It is a process which has been written about countless times. Its short and long term repercussions – economic, political and social – have been and still are debated by academics. The focus, particularly among social historians, has been on the people of the rapidly growing towns and cities. This is understandable as it was there that the cotton mills and the factories made Britain the 'workshop of the world'. It was in these places that the new forms of industrial organisation and new ways of working and living (and dying) were being experienced most directly and by the greatest numbers.

The consequences of the industrial revolution for the life and landscape of rural Britain have been less well documented. It is true that large swathes of the countryside would eventually be swallowed by the expanding urban areas. Many villages and hamlets survived, however, and continue to do so. Yet they would not survive unaltered. The shape and character of some villages were drastically redrawn by the advances and innovations in transport that were a fundamental part of the industrial revolution. And the people living in these rural communities were not immune to the historical shifts and transitions which swept the country during the 18th and 19th centuries. They may not have felt the effects as immediately as their brothers and sisters in the towns, and sometimes they were affected in different ways, but they did not escape them.

There is a village that as a child I used to visit with my parents. It held a special fascination for me and I would look forward to going there. I wanted to know why it had certain features – a canal bridge here, an entrance to a railway tunnel there – that other places didn't and why they were sited where they were. The *when?* questions didn't register until my interest in history was kindled quite late in my school career by a new and enthusiastic young teacher. It was also only then that I began to realise that the really interesting history was not about a bunch of some far distant kings and queens and battles but about ordinary people going about their everyday lives and work. As Stephen Fry has put it, they are us – '*had we been born a little earlier*'[1]. The popularity of *reality television* indicates our fascination with what others are up to now. And judging by other TV programmes – whether they be tracing family histories, digging up (sometimes literally) evidence of past ways of life, or even dramatised versions of actual events set in a village, town, factory or farm of some previous age – what might be called reality history seems to appeal to many viewers, too. But even when university channelled my history studies along more formal lines, the *when?* questions were invariably of less importance than the *why?* – indeed they were only important if they helped to answer the *why*.

Despite what the novelist L P Hartley would have us believe, the past may not be a foreign country – but it is a vast one. So to the *why?*, *who?* and *when?* questions, should be added the *what?*: what to include, what to leave out. The academic study of history of necessity requires the discipline of sticking to what is immediately relevant. And because of specialisation, what is of immediate relevance to the academic historian will be essentially narrow. It was liberating, therefore, to come across Bill Bryson's *At Home: A Short History of Private Life*. Unencumbered by the boundary constraints of the formal historian, Bryson uses each of the rooms of his house to explore whatever seemingly random bits of history take his fancy. He gives us histories of crop rotation and furniture design, provides entertaining glimpses into the invention of the mousetrap and the origins of the principles of architecture, and allows his readers to link the discovery of a prehistoric human body to the redundant buttons on jacket cuffs. His book serves to demonstrate how, in Lenin's phrase, *'everything is connected with everything else'*. Often the connections will be far from obvious, just as glances through the window of a train or car journey present us with apparently unrelated frames of life and landscape, frozen in time. Yet if we were to walk the same route and observe closely, the relationships between the frames would become clearer, the picture more fluid.

In moving effortlessly from ancient Rome to the 1851 Great Exhibition and back again or from the blackout of the Second World War to the activities of Samuel Pepys, Bryson also reminds us that it is not always necessary or desirable to represent history chronologically. This is not to deny that an understanding of sequence is important – to be aware that the Romans in Britain preceded the Saxons, for example, or that the First World War came after the South African War. Time-lines can be very useful, even indispensable, but presenting history, in the words of Cambridge Professor Sir Herbert Butterfield, as *'just one bloody thing after another'* can be so dispiriting if it becomes its sole or main purpose.

The story that unfolds in these pages, then, does not do so in a strictly linear fashion, but there are dates and it does move through five generations. The five generations are of one family but the story is not only about one family. It is about the history of a particular village but it is not only about one village. It is also about key elements of a crucial period in Britain's history, a period of rapid and unprecedented economic and social change. It is about the reasons behind the changes and about their direct and indirect effects at the time and over the years following – to the First World War and beyond. Enjoy the journey.

THE SPROSTON FAMILY

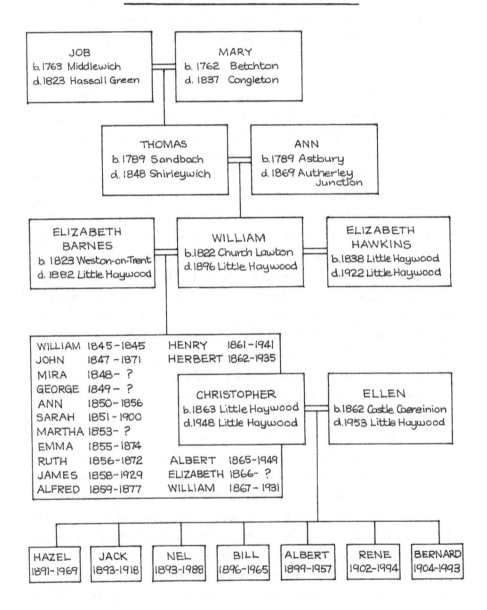

JOB
b. 1763 Middlewich
d. 1823 Hassall Green

MARY
b. 1762 Betchton
d. 1837 Congleton

THOMAS
b. 1789 Sandbach
d. 1848 Shirleywich

ANN
b. 1789 Astbury
d. 1869 Autherley Junction

ELIZABETH BARNES
b. 1823 Weston-on-Trent
d. 1882 Little Haywood

WILLIAM
b. 1822 Church Lawton
d. 1896 Little Haywood

ELIZABETH HAWKINS
b. 1838 Little Haywood
d. 1922 Little Haywood

WILLIAM 1845–1845
JOHN 1847–1871
MIRA 1848–?
GEORGE 1849–?
ANN 1850–1856
SARAH 1851–1900
MARTHA 1853–?
EMMA 1855–1874
RUTH 1856–1872
JAMES 1858–1929
ALFRED 1859–1877

HENRY 1861–1941
HERBERT 1862–1935

CHRISTOPHER
b. 1863 Little Haywood
d. 1948 Little Haywood

ELLEN
b. 1862 Castle Caereinion
d. 1953 Little Haywood

ALBERT 1865–1949
ELIZABETH 1866–?
WILLIAM 1867–1931

HAZEL
1891–1969

JACK
1893–1918

NEL
1893–1988

BILL
1896–1965

ALBERT
1899–1957

RENE
1902–1994

BERNARD
1904–1993

TRENT & MERSEY CANAL

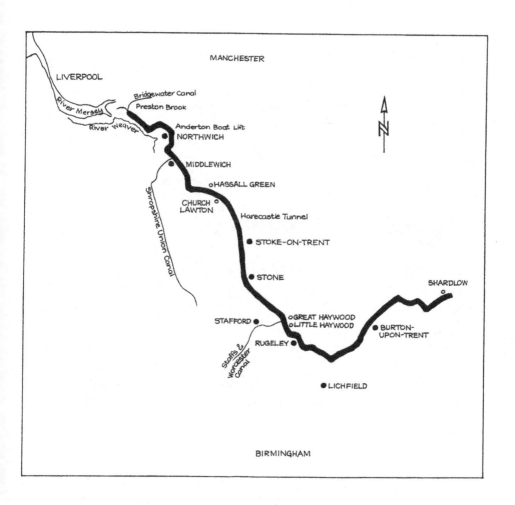

THE VILLAGES TODAY

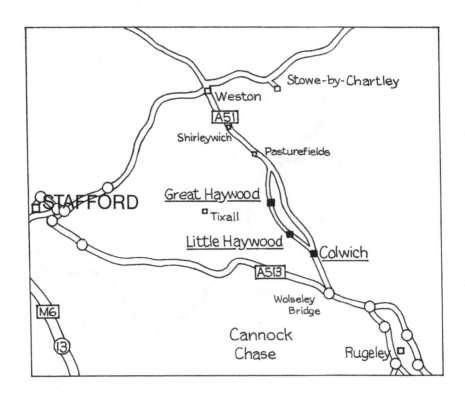

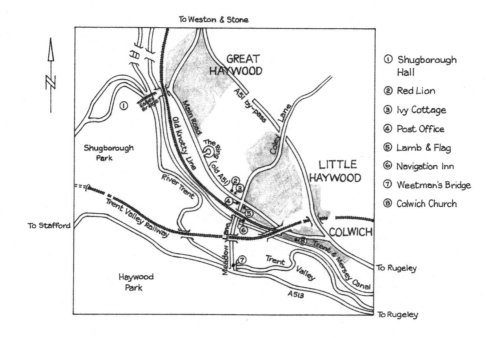

To Weston & Stone

GREAT HAYWOOD

A51 by-pass

Coley Lane

LITTLE HAYWOOD

Shugborough Park

Main Road

Old Knotty Line

The Ring (old A51)

River Trent

Trent Valley Railway

To Stafford

COLWICH

To Rugeley

Meadow Lane

Trent Valley

Trent & Mersey Canal

Haywood Park

A513

To Rugeley

① Shugborough Hall
② Red Lion
③ Ivy Cottage
④ Post Office
⑤ Lamb & Flag
⑥ Navigation Inn
⑦ Weetman's Bridge
⑧ Colwich Church

Chapter 1

William the Farmer and Innkeeper… and Elizabeth I

Nel was not there when it happened, but she wasn't far away. The damage was extensive: five wounds to the head, right ear almost severed, fractured left collar bone, ribs broken on right side, internal injuries…

It was a late winter's day. The driver was on the main route through the village where he had lived and worked for more than 30 years. To avoid a pile of stone chippings he moved over to the wrong side. Seconds before, and from the opposite direction, the butcher had lost control of his vehicle. It careered down the hill.

The collision was severe. The first driver was thrown into the road. His heavy cargo followed, crushing him against the hard ground. It was a serious road traffic accident. The inquest heard that William Sproston's death resulted from 'shock to the system' caused by the horrific injuries he sustained. William was 74.

He had not been killed outright. His bleeding and broken body was carried the short distance back to his home, The Navigation Inn. There, according to the local paper, he 'expired' a few hours later. An account of how William's pony and trap came to be hit by another is reported in some detail. So, too, is the verdict of accidental death: no one was to blame. The condition of the ponies is not recorded[1].

To her family, Eleanor Mary Sproston was always Nel. She lived with her mother, father and two brothers, including twin Jack, in the same village – just up the road. She knew her grandfather well. But she would not remember him for Nel was barely three years old when she last saw him. William died on 16 March 1896 – just five months before Britain's first ever recorded road death from a motor accident. The casualty was a middle-aged woman out for a stroll in south-east London, run over by the young driver of a Roger-Benz motor car[2]. In the years since, over 32 million people have died in road traffic accidents worldwide[3].

Yet the motorised conveyance was only the latest in a series of advances in transport that had played an important role in William's life and those of his ancestors. These developments have also shaped many of the contours within which modern life takes place: where we live and whom we live with, where we work and where we play, what we buy, whom we talk to and why, and what we talk about.

The car that ended the life of that unfortunate pedestrian had been travelling at 4 mph. Although the report of William's accident contains no reference to speed, the impact of a downhill bolting horse pulling one trap and colliding with another would have been greater. In any event, it was a grisly end not only to William's life but to a successful career. Or, rather, careers, for by the time of his death William had been a farmer, a publican, a milkman, a coal merchant and an owner of canal boats – and all of these, at least for a period, at the same time.

William was born in 1822 – probably; and to a family of possibly a dozen children. There are reasons for this lack of precision. National registration of births in England and Wales did not begin until 1837 and, before the law was tightened in 1875, as many as a fifth of births may not have been registered in this way[4]. Family historians wishing to find information prior to civil (as opposed to Church) registration, turn to parish records but these are not comprehensive and often give the date of baptism, rather than birth. It is known that William was baptised on 3 January 1823 in Church Lawton, a small village on the Cheshire-Staffordshire border. Little is known of his childhood but at some stage in the late 1820s, the family moved across the county boundary to an area of Staffordshire where, despite changing residence, and village, a number of times, William was to spend the rest of his life.

It was here he met a local girl, the daughter of a general labourer, who had been working with an older sister at one of the village pubs. At the age of 21, and three months pregnant with their first child, she became Elizabeth the First when she married William who was a year or two older. William was making a living as a cordwainer (a shoemaker or leather worker) at the time[5]. It was not long, however, before census returns were listing him in a rather different line of work: in keeping with family tradition he was now a canal boatman. He had been brought up on the boats and knew the ropes. So, shortly after his marriage, William ceased making shoes and became a boatman in his own right.

Diversification into coal and milk distribution was to come later but by his early forties William was running a public house and he became a farmer at the same time or shortly after. The business skills he was to pick up, though, were not due to any formal education. At least at the time of his marriage to Elizabeth, William was illiterate. When, on 1 February 1845, they were married at Baswich's Holy Trinity Church, close to the Staffordshire and Worcestershire Canal, he could not sign his name in the register. There was no national system of schooling in England and Wales before the 1870s. The proportion of people signing, as opposed to making a mark, on marriage certificates before that time is sometimes taken to indicate the rate of literacy[6]. Using this measure, it has been suggested that up to 80% of the adult population could read and write even before the days of mass education[7]. It is one thing to learn to sign one's own name in advance of your wedding, however, but quite another to be able to read a newspaper or to write a letter – so such claims are likely to be highly exaggerated. Nonetheless, the reverse – not even being able to produce a signature – can be regarded as reasonable evidence of illiteracy. (In Elizabethan times, for some people it was fashionable to use a mark on official documents even if they could read and write[8], but this affectation did not extend to Victorian times.)

The image of William that reaches us today is of a wiry, possibly quite restless, certainly active man who was unafraid of change. His lack of education did not prevent him from embracing a widening range of business interests. But although, in the second half of his life, there would be paid employees as well as members of his family working for him, he nonetheless maintained a decidedly hands-on involvement in the day-to-day activities of his businesses. And this continued right up to – and including – the day he died. At the time of the accident William had been transporting large sacks of corn[9].

Evidently, he was a busy man – but not as busy as Elizabeth, who, between 1845 and 1867, bore their seventeen children.

(Family lore has it that she actually gave birth twenty-one times, so presumably some were still-born.) Large families were not unusual in the pre-Welfare State days of Victorian England: a third of all families had more than seven children[10]. As in those countries of the 20th and early 21st century with no or little state social security, having many children operated as a family insurance scheme: at least some children were likely to survive and be able to look after parents who became too old or sick to provide for themselves.

Yet giving birth to seventeen or more children was not common. It must have been difficult for the Sprostons to keep track of the names of the ten sons and seven daughters. Perhaps this is why the first and last born were both called William, after their father. The more likely reason for the duplication, though, is that their first child lived for only a few days. Although Ann, the fifth born, died before her sixth birthday, all the others lived at least into adolescence (and most for considerably longer). The high childhood survival rate, particularly in very large families, was unusual for the Victorian era. In the mid-nineteenth century, half of all children did not live long enough to become adults. The major causes of childhood deaths were measles, whooping cough, diphtheria and scarlet fever (the last, in particular, often spread through contaminated milk)[11]. The high incidence of child deaths (and in the first year of life in particular) meant that life expectancy rates at birth were spectacularly low compared with today. Although the situation was to improve quite noticeably by the end of the century, the rates among the poorer classes and in some of the large industrial towns and cities in the mid-1800s reflected the harsh, overcrowded and insanitary living conditions in which disease thrived and spread rapidly. In the heavily industrialised Black Country town of Dudley, barely 20 miles from William's village, life expectancy hit a low of just 18.5 years[12]. A report of 1852 labelled it *the most unhealthy place in the country*[13] – not one of the more appealing straplines to use on your 'Welcome to Dudley' signs, especially as a 2011 national 'happy at home' survey ranked it top town for 'well-being' and 'pride'[14]. It is unlikely that such accolades would have been accorded 160 years earlier: with a teenage life expectancy, people just would not have had the time to complete life-style questionnaires.

For the Sproston family, the relatively good fortune in surviving childhood did not continue for long. The 1870s was an especially cruel decade. Between 1871 and 1877, Elizabeth and William saw four more of their offspring (three of them still in their teenage years) into an early grave. In each case the death was recorded as *phthisis* – or 'wasting disease'[15]. The most likely cause of this would have been pulmonary tuberculosis, although it was not until 1882 that the German microbiologist, Robert Koch, discovered the tubercle bacillus. The consumption of raw milk then soon became recognised as a major source of transmission of tuberculosis in general. The disease has since been described as *'the single greatest cause of death and disability in nineteenth century Britain'*[16].

The 1870s was not a happy time for many people in the countryside. Abnormally wet weather hampered crop cultivation and reduced the quality of milk in dairy farming[17]. There were poor harvests in seven of the ten years and the decade also saw the start of what came to be called by some earlier historians the Great Depression in agriculture (and dated, rather precisely, as 1873-1896). All branches of farming in Britain – and elsewhere in the Western world – were affected as an increase in global food supplies led to falling prices, profits and rents[18]. But some sectors – mainly cereal production – fared worse than others, such as dairy.

And, indeed, it was the land-owning and business classes with interests in large scale arable (crop production) farming which tended to be the most vociferous complainers about the downturn in their economic fortunes[19, 20]. Yet, overall, real wages and general living standards in Britain were rising. More recent interpretations of this era point to a restructuring of the agricultural economy, rather than a depression[21]. To survive, farmers often had to switch from the declining sectors of production, such as cereal crops, to more profitable ventures such as fruit growing and market gardening. And although mixed farming was still common[22], the switch from arable (wheat acreage declined by half between 1791 and 1901) to pasture for raising livestock (cattle and sheep) gathered apace[23, 24].

This is not to say that tenant farmers and agricultural workers, even in the relatively more favoured branches of farming, escaped unscathed, however. Nationally there was an increase in rural unemployment. And the changes taking place on the land, as farming attempted to adjust to steeply falling cereal prices in particular[25], disrupted the lives of many of those who relied on agriculture to provide for themselves and their families. Thousands of smaller farms went under, the number of people engaged in farm work shrank and rural depopulation became a feature of the last few decades of the 19th century[26]. In William's parish, for example, the population of the villages fell by nearly one-third between 1851 and 1901, and the proportion of the occupied workforce engaged in agriculture in 1881 was markedly down on what it had been 50 years earlier[27]. The decline continued: in England and Wales as a whole, the number of hired farm workers fell by one-third over the 40 years from 1871[28]. For those adversely affected by the events and changes of the latter decades of the 19th century, fine distinctions between *depression* and *restructuring* would have been purely academic.

Perhaps at least partly because William's income was not dependent solely on his farm, this branch of his business survived. Yet personal tragedy continued. Five years after the death of the fourth child in six years, Elizabeth herself died; she was in her late fifties. After bearing and caring for 17 children, losing six of them, helping to run the pub where they lived, and the daily drudgery of looking after such a large household, this is hardly surprising. What was The Navigation Inn is today a very pleasant, detached canal-side cottage, ideal for the size of the modern family. The 1871 census lists 16 people living there: William and Elizabeth, 12 of their children (two of whom by this time adults) and two farm labourers. As the public house part of the business would have taken up at least some of the ground floor, the sleeping and general living arrangements were somewhat on the cramped side.

With large families and small cottages, the overcrowded living conditions of agricultural workers' families were far from unusual. An article in The Cornhill Magazine in 1874 noted:

'The cottage… is, in many of our rural districts, … a scandal and disgrace to England. We could point to village after village, and name them by their names, in which there are houses inhabited by whole families, in which there is but one bed-room; many with only a sort of outer lobby or landing which serves as a room, and one only regular 'chamber; three rooms are quite an exception in almost all our older village tenements. The sanitary arrangements are in keeping, and even ordinary personal cleanliness is out of the question.'[29]

In addition, the 19th century witnessed changes which affected the stability of housing provision previous generations of agricultural workers may have enjoyed. Increasingly, farm labour was being hired by the week or the day with no obligation on employers to provide accommodation. But even where the tied cottage system prevailed, security of tenure was linked to the job: lose your job and the cottage could be lost, too[30]. And, with the changes in agricultural production and fluctuations in trade making casual labour hire increasingly attractive to landowners and farmers, the position of the tied cottager was becoming more insecure.

Arguably, though, the living conditions and the scale of overcrowding – to say nothing of security of accommodation – were often worse in some of the rapidly expanding towns and cities of Britain, including certain districts of London. A priest in Bethnal Green described how, in his parish of under 400 yards square, 12,000 people were crammed into 1,400 houses

'… and in this overcrowding it is nothing unusual to find a man, his wife four or five children, and, sometimes, both grandparents, all in one single room of ten to twelve square feet, where they eat, sleep, and work… Not one father of a family in ten in the whole neighbourhood has other clothing than his working suit, and that is as bad and tattered as possible; many indeed have no other covering

for the night than these rags, and no bed, save a sack of straw and shavings.'[31]

In Glasgow, meanwhile, the deprivations, the housing density and the consequent health risks, if anything could be even greater:

> *'There are numbers of ... localities in the heart of the city [which contain] endless labyrinths of lanes or wynds into which open at almost every step, courts or blind alleys, formed by ill-ventilated, high-piled, waterless, and dilapidated houses. These are literally swarming with inhabitants. They contain three or four families upon each floor, perhaps twenty persons. In some cases each storey is let out in sleeping places, so that fifteen to twenty persons are packed, one on top of the other, I cannot say accommodated, in a single room. These districts ... may be regarded as the sources of those frightful epidemics which ... spread desolation over Glasgow.'*[32]

The existence of teeming, insanitary, airless courts housing huge numbers of people in very close proximity was not confined to the nation's older cities. As a feature of 19th century urban working class life, they extended to the new or vastly expanded manufacturing towns of the industrial revolution. Manchester gained city status in 1853 after its population had more than tripled in just fifty years on the back of the explosive growth of the cotton industry. In the 1840s, after moving there from Germany to train in the running of his family's textile business, Frederick Engels made close observations of areas of his adopted town for his pioneering work *The Condition of the Working Class in England.* He noted that in a district by the River Irk, for example:

> *'Right and left a multitude of covered passages lead from the main street into numerous courts, and he who turns in thither gets into a filth and disgusting grime, the equal of which is not to be found – especially in the courts which lead down to the Irk, and which contain unqualifiedly the most horrible dwellings which I have yet beheld. In one of these courts there stands directly at the entrance ...*

a privy without a door, so dirty that the inhabitants can pass into and out of the court only by passing through foul pools of stagnant urine and excrement. This is the first court on the Irk above Ducie Bridge – in case anyone should care to look into it. Below it on the river there are several tanneries, which fill the whole neighbourhood with the stench of animal putrefaction. Below Ducie Bridge the only entrance to most of the houses is by means of narrow, dirty stairs and over heaps of refuse and filth… Above the bridge are tanneries, bone mills, and gas works, from which all drains and refuse find their way into the Irk, which receives further the contents of all the neighbouring … privies. It may be easily imagined, therefore, what sort of residue the stream deposits.'[33]

Judging by rental listings and the reports of public health authorities and Poor Law medical officers in various parts of the country, the situation does not seem to have improved by the 1860s. A listing of houses from a dozen or so streets in Bradford, for instance, indicates that it was not rare for more than 10 people to be sharing one room or for seven or eight people to be living in a cellar. One example gives 18 persons living in one room in George Street while a room in the house next door allowed rather more spacious living for only 16[34]. Elsewhere in the town, one small group of streets was home for 1,450 with just 36 privies among them[35].

To compare 19th century urban living conditions with those in the countryside is not to suggest, however, that village life was the sort of rural idyll that is sometimes portrayed today. Accommodation for the typical farm worker and his family was often basic, damp, poorly maintained and, as has been shown, frequently insanitary and too small for the number of people housed within. One writer paints a picture of:

'… large families liv[ing] in one or two rooms, with earth floors that "heaved" and [which] were sometimes awash in winter with damp or even flowing with spring water. Neither roof nor walls were rain-proof, dirt and droppings oozed from the thatch, and water had to be fetched in from a pond, pump or rain barrel. One or two privies at the end of the garden might have to serve for eight or ten families.' [36]

Despite the exceptional size of William's household, there would have been many families in his village a good deal worse off. And, at least by the later part of the century, there are indications that the Sprostons' cramped living conditions were not necessarily an indicator of financial poverty or a lack of wealth – as Will's will will reveal.

Chapter 2

The Village and Elizabeth 2

£1,660,000 seems like a lot of money. It is a lot of money. It is, according to one method of calculation, the amount of William's estate in today's value. According to another, however, it is £161,000 – still not to be sniffed at, but less than one-tenth of the first estimate.

These two amounts represent the highest and the lowest of a range of values based on different ways of working out monetary equivalences over different periods[1]. The actual amount left by William – 'farmer, innkeeper and coal dealer' – in 1896 was £1,782.14s.8d[2] (or £1,782. 73 expressed in post-1971 decimal currency). No single measure of equivalence is entirely satisfactory, however. For example, the lowest value is calculated on the cost of buying the same basket of goods at today's prices compared with the prices in 1896. The problem here, though, is that the typical shopping basket of today would contain many items that were not around 115 years ago: ready-meals, TV magazines, memory sticks, dishwasher tablets. And that is even before we think of the more occasional purchases of microwave ovens, televisions, computers and dishwashers.

But whatever the real worth of the estate at his death, the chief beneficiary appears to have been Elizabeth the Second. Two years after the death of the first Elizabeth, William had remarried. Elizabeth Hawkins had been born in the village and was well known to William and his family. She was a near neighbour who kept a local shop and she was with William's son, John, when he died in 1871[3]. Elizabeth 2 was the third of seven children of wheelwright Thomas Hawkins and his wife Elizabeth (a locally popular forename, it seems). And, had they still been around, William would have no problem remembering the first names of his new in-laws: they were the same as the first.

At the time of his second marriage – the wedding took place at a church in Aston, Birmingham in May 1884 – William would have been 62 years old. His age on the certificate, though, is given as 59. Whether this is an indication of vanity, a desire to narrow the appearance of the age gap between himself and his new wife – who was 45 – or merely an example of the apparently cavalier attitude to age declarations on official documents that prevailed before the 20th century, must remain an open question. But this time around, William is able to sign his own name. He may have learned to do this especially for the occasion, however, for he was still using an X only a few years earlier[4].

If Elizabeth 2 ever sat in her bedroom pondering her wealth, the scene from her window at the Navigation Inn in Little Haywood would not have been far different from what it is now – though with fewer coniferous trees on the skyline. The large outbuilding at the front would have then partially restricted the vista to the south. But with the barn long since removed, the full beauty of the panorama is revealed. With the rest of the village on rising ground to the rear of the house, from the front there is a barely interrupted view across the lush pastureland of the Trent Valley towards the ancient forest of Cannock Chase, itself a designated Area of Outstanding Natural Beauty. To the west lies the impressive landscaped parkland of Shugborough Hall. An 18th century visitor was enchanted:

'I must imagine the traveller, as well as myself, blinded, if we rode this space insensible of the most elegant view of the vale. It is perfectly prodigal in its beauties, and spreads at once every charm that can captivate the eye.'[5]

Navigation Inn about 1910 [Courtesy of The Haywood Society collection]

*...and today, with canal in foreground and overhead gantry of
the electrified railway line at rear*

With little visual change since, the same could still be said. It is hardly surprising, therefore, that the village should appeal to the modern urbanite in search of a more tranquil home life. With a 2001 combined population approaching 2,500 – 70% up on 1931[6] – Little Haywood and its close neighbour Colwich are now established dormitory villages. They serve not only the nearby towns of Stafford and Rugeley but, courtesy of the motorway network, much further afield, too.

Compared with the varied job opportunities of the first half of the 20th century, though, there is now little local employment[7]. In the early 1900s, the locality could boast a great variety of trades and crafts people, including: brewer, brick layer, brick maker, three coal merchants, cooper, inland revenue officer, miller, saddle and harness maker, shoemaker, and various shopkeepers and shop workers[8]. In 1928, a sub-branch of a bank opened in Little Haywood and by 1936 the local farm machinery contractor had expanded into 'motor haulage', reflecting the spread of car ownership[9]. Add to this list a midwife, a district nurse, a couple of doctors, railway employees, various school teachers, a dog-breeder and, as you might expect from a rural area of the period, smallholders, a market gardener, nurseryman and 25 farmers[10], and the rich social and economic diversity of village life contrasts sharply with the modern dormitory village's much narrower ranges of social class, income and age. Over the past 30 years, young people with families have been increasingly priced out of the local private housing sector. And the declining stock of local authority housing often means that the current descendants of successive generations of the same village families are forced to seek accommodation and work elsewhere. In the 15th and 16th centuries, it was the changing patterns of land ownership that forced working families from the countryside; today it is the housing market.

Little Haywood is one of a group of recognisably distinct but inter-connected villages where William Sproston had spent most of his life and where he had brought up his large family. It forms part of the parish of Colwich which also gives its name to the village which adjoins Little Haywood to the South-East. A railway line now acts as a boundary separating the two communities but the road passing beneath allows services and facilities to be shared. Little Haywood has no church but Colwich is home to the ancient St Michael and All Angels in whose churchyard lie Sprostons from different generations. Today neither village hosts a bank, post office or medical practice but a mobile library visits both villages on alternate Tuesdays. There is a primary school in Colwich but no school in Little Haywood. On the other hand the thirsty villagers of Colwich – which at one time had 16 alehouses[11] – today have to walk to the Lamb & Flag (a listed building) or the Red Lion, both in Little Haywood. These two pubs are just a few yards from each other on opposite sides of the main road in the centre of the village[12].

William and his family would have known both establishments (the current Red Lion, rebuilt in the 1930s, occupies the same site as the original). Not only were they just a short stroll away, to some extent they would also have been competitors to their own public house. The Navigation Inn was built in Meadow Lane which leads out, in a southerly direction, from the centre of Little Haywood towards the river and to Cannock Chase beyond. At the far end of the lane, just before it enters the A513 Stafford road, there is an attractive single-carriageway stone bridge spanning the river. This is Weetman's Bridge, which still has a cobbled road surface. Built in 1887, it would have proved of special benefit to William in his remaining years for it replaced the previous wooden footbridge which had existed for more than half a century[13]. Before the construction of the stone bridge, William would have had to drive his cattle and any horse-drawn vehicles across the adjacent ford to reach those of his fields on the south side of the river.

Weetman's Bridge, Little Haywood, photographed a few years after its construction in 1887. [Courtesy of Mrs L Davies]

If Colwich lies to one side of Little Haywood, immediately on the opposite side is Great Haywood. The name 'Haywood' comes from the Old English 'haeg wudu' – an 'enclosed wood'[14] or possibly 'an enclosure in a wooded area'. It appears in Domesday Book as 'Haiwode' and described as 'land for 10 ploughs' held by the Bishop of Chester[15]. The 'Great' and 'Little' epithets are thought to originate not from any difference in the size of the settlements, but to the different densities of the immediately surrounding wooded areas[16]. The two Haywoods are separated physically only by a sandstone outcrop called 'The Butts'[17]. This forms the hill down which charged the runaway pony that led to William's unfortunate accident.

A little over two miles to the north lies the hamlet of Shirleywich, just one mile south of the village of Weston. These settlements, together with the Haywoods and Colwich, all lie in that part of Staffordshire that still retains a rural flavour despite being geographically close to the large industrial conurbations of the Black Country to the south and the pottery towns around Stoke-on-Trent to the north. Through or close by each of the villages, flows the Trent, Britain's third longest river.

Culturally and historically, the Trent has divided the North of England from the South[18]. Sections of the river may have been navigated as early as the Bronze Age[19] and, centuries later, the Romans called The Trent 'Trisantona'. Their early settlements did not extend beyond its southern boundary but it is known that a Roman cohort was stationed at what is now Wolseley Bridge, a hamlet half-a-mile to the south-east of Colwich[20]. In the 7th century, the Celts negotiated the river as far as what became Stone (a few miles to the north of the villages) which Wulfhere, King of Mercia established as his capital[21]. Two hundred years later, the Viking invasion was aided by using the Trent to penetrate westwards, venturing within a couple of miles of the villages[22]. During the Civil War, a number of battles were fought close to the river including that at Hopton Heath (just up the road from Weston) in 1643. The outcome of this battle was inconclusive despite the royalist commander, the Earl of Northampton, being one of an estimated 400 men (from both sides) to lose their lives[23]. In the days leading up to the battle, there were related clashes between the two sides at Little Haywood when the royalist army attempted to see off parliamentary troops encamped there[24, 25].

The Trent's life begins to the north of Stoke from where it wends its way southwards for the first part of its journey. At Great Haywood, on the eastern side of Shugborough Hall, it widens at Essex Bridge where it is met by its first major tributary, the River Sow (the Sow, in turn, having been fed a little further upstream by the Penk)[26]. The bridge today is a fascinating Grade 1 listed structure of 14 arches and is wide enough only to accommodate foot (or hoof) traffic and with very low sides and passing places every few yards. There is uncertainty about when it was first constructed but at one time it had at least 40 arches, extending into Shugborough Park[27]. But even with its much reduced span, it is still recorded as the longest remaining packhorse bridge in Britain[28, 29].

Initially named the Shugborough Bridge, the legend is that it was built so that Queen Elizabeth I, when staying with the Earl of

Essex at his nearby estate at Chartley Castle, could cross the river to deer-hunt on Cannock Chase[30, 31]. Although the Earl may well have overseen structural repairs to ensure the safety of his royal visitor, records suggest that the original bridge, probably at least partly of a wooden structure, pre-dates this period[32].

Standing on the centre of the bridge one day in 1780, a guest at Shugborough Hall described a view:

> *'of very uncommon beauty, of a small vale, varied with almost everything that nature or art could give to render it delicious; rich meadows watered by the Trent and Sow. The first animated with milk-white cattle…; the last with numerous swans. The boundary on one side, is a cultivated slope; on the other, the lofty front of Cannck Wood, clothed with heath or shaded with old oaks, scattered over its glowing bloom by the free hand of nature.'[33]*

One hundred and thirty-six years later, the bridge itself, and even possibly the chimneys of Shugborough Hall, may have been the inspiration for J R R Tolkien's city of Tavrobel in *The Book of Lost Tales*. As one river traveller wryly observes, it is 'just the kind of bridge that would find its way into a rigmarole about elves and gnomes and the ancient days'[34]. The famous author did indeed know the area. During part of his First World War army days, he was stationed on Cannock Chase and lived for six months with his wife in lodgings at Great Haywood. After fighting on the Somme and contracting trench fever, it was there he recuperated and began writing some of his early tales[35].

The nearest town downstream of the villages is Rugeley where the giant cooling towers of the power station form a prominent feature of the landscape. Supplying the National Grid with electricity for half-a-million homes[36], Rugeley B power station, opened in 1972, takes vast volumes of water from the Trent, as did Meaford power station near Stone until it ceased operation in 1990. There is a three-mile stretch of the river below Stoke where effluent discharges make the quality of the water the worst of the entire river[37]. Otherwise the river runs through towns with arguably some of the best drinking water in the country. It is no accident that Burton-on-Trent has been and remains, as the town's distinctive smell testifies, a major centre for the brewing industry. The secret apparently lies in the high gypsum content of the area's water supply[38]. On a smaller scale, Stone – which has a thousand years of brewing history – produced some fine beers including, until closure of the brewery in the 1970s, the renown and much missed Joule's bitter.

The Trent has been an important trade route from the Black Country, via the Ouse and Humber to the North Sea[39]. But the section that flows through the villages is not important commercially today as the river is not continuously navigable until beyond Shardlow to the east of Burton-upon-Trent, some miles downstream. It has been significant, though, in establishing the nature of farming – the well-irrigated, verdant corridor of land being particularly suitable for grazing – and thereby the livelihoods of the villagers for many generations. There are records of large-scale dairy farming at the Haywoods in the 13th century and of sheep grazing from the early 14th century[40]. Water, a plentiful supply of timber and good pasture made this area of the Trent valley ideal for early settlements[41]. Its historical importance for the locality is revealed in the names of three nearby hamlets which all carry the name Ridware, or 'river people'[42].

Today, although there is mixed farming, pasture still predominates as flooding in the fields closest to the river restricts cultivation[43]. Although a farm machinery contractor operated from nearby Wolseley Bridge in the first half of the 20th century, the demand for his services was hardly stretched. Mechanisation was slow to reach the farms in the villages. It was not until after the Second World War that the noise of tractors, hedge trimmers, milking machines and combine harvesters would become an accepted part of the soundtrack to local village life. The horse-power of the machine age was at last replacing the 'horse and man' power of traditional agriculture[44].

It was not the river, however, which was responsible for the early 19th century Sproston family move from Cheshire to Staffordshire – but a rather different form of waterway and, underlying that, a historical development of monumental proportions.

Chapter 3

An Age of Revolution: The Journeys Start

The beginnings of the Sproston family journey lie in Middlewich, a Cheshire town of Roman origin just over 20 miles south of Manchester. This is where, in 1763, William Sproston's grandfather (and Nel's great-great-grandfather), Job, was born.

Job's ancestors had lived there for at least the best part of two centuries, and probably much longer. His great-great grandparents, John and Alice, had both been born there in the late 1620s and it is possible that so, too, had John's mother. There is also a likely family connection to a Ralph Sproston, 'yeoman of Middlewich', who died in 1617[1]. As youngsters, John and Alice might well have witnessed one or both of the two Civil War Battles of Middlewich which took place in 1643. Although Parliamentarian forces controlled the Middlewich area for most of the war, successfully deposing the Royalists at the first battle in March, they lost 200 men during the second battle nine months later[2].

It has been claimed that a group of poor families from Middlewich 'took advantage' of the disruptions of the Civil War by breaking into and occupying the recently opened House of Correction[3]. Certainly, a warrant was issued by Justices at the Cheshire Quarter Sessions in 1645 ordering the constables of Middlewich to evict:

> 'diverse persons [who] (taking occasion by the present distractions) have broken into and possessed themselves of the said House, there intending to inhabit and dwell, by which means the same house and diverse utensils... are spoiled and kept from the use intended, and rogues, lewd and dissolute persons much encouraged in their idle lewd courses, to the great detriment and terror of the Country...'[4]

This, and repeated warrants of a similar nature over the following two years, appears to have had little effect, however, and the House of Correction continued to be occupied. Perhaps keenly aware of the upheavals to people's lives that wars invariably incur – including homelessness and loss of livelihood – the actions of the squatters apparently drew sympathy from the townspeople. This included the local constables themselves who, it seems, ignored the magistrates' orders and were stripped of their law-enforcing roles as a result[5].

Among the small number of occupiers identified by name in the court's warrants is an Elizabeth Sprosten, a widow who, a few years later, is listed in local records as in receipt of parish poor relief[6]. Records do not reveal if Elizabeth was directly connected to John Sproston but some family relationship seems possible. Rare as a surname nationally, there is still a comparative profusion of Sprostons in Cheshire[7] and it is probable that the origin of the name has a geographical connection to this part of the county in particular. Domesday Book includes the settlement of Sprostune[8]. In 1086 it was a small village little more than a stone's throw from Middlewich (or Mildestvich). Today, Sproston is a small village – or more precisely hamlet (for there is no church) – little more than a stone's throw from Middlewich, and close to junction 18 of the M6 motorway. It has no village hall or shop but it does have a pub, The Fox and Hounds, and boasts a parish council with five councillors and a clerk (none of whom is currently a Sproston)[9].

Job Sproston became a boat builder, living and working in the Rode Heath/Odd Rode/Hassall Green area – a dozen miles south-east of Middlewich, but still in Cheshire. His career was interrupted in his late forties by a spell of imprisonment in Chester Castle. He lived on to the age of 60, however, dying not long after grandson William's birth. Job and wife Mary had a number of children including Thomas (William's father) who also became a boat builder and boatman.

Thomas Sproston's lifespan was framed exactly by the 'age of revolution', 1789-1848. This is the historian E J Hobsbawm's phrase to define both the political upheavals in France and the industrial transformations in England: a cataclysmic period which was to change fundamentally the course of European and global history[10]. Thomas was born in the year of the storming of the Bastille and died, in 1848, at the time of another turbulent episode in French history.

His final breath, however, was drawn not on the bloody streets of Paris but on the more peaceful waters of rural Staffordshire[11]. His entire life had been spent on and with canal boats: living on them, working them, building them. Boats have been made and used for thousands of years. But the type of boat – the canal narrowboat – which Thomas and his father built, was new. It was related directly to the great industrial and economic changes in England to which Hobsbawm refers.

These were the changes of the industrial revolution. Over a period of up to a hundred years, from the mid to late-1700s to the mid-1800s, Britain became the first country to undergo a process that would completely transform the whole of society and, eventually, the entire world. The effects of the industrial revolution would do more than touch the lives of those around at the time. Its consequences were so widespread and so profound that, over just a few generations, almost every aspect of the way people lived their lives, and at every stage of their lives, would be changed. And it still defines the way we, as human and social beings, organise our lives today.

There were, of course, certain continuities and the speed of change would appear faster in the towns and cities than in the rural areas. If Job Sproston, who had died in 1823, had been able to visit Little Haywood's Navigation Inn and to see his grandson's farm and his grandson's boats, he might well have felt very much at home. At least on the surface, many things would have looked familiar. But if we were to stretch the generations at each end – so that Job's father was transported into the adult lives of Nel and of William's other grandchildren – the picture, would be very different. And for those living in, or moving to, the rapidly growing urban areas of the 19th century, the luxury of time to adjust to the changes would not be on offer. The industrial revolution would hit, and hit hard, within one and the same generation.

Most adults in Britain today will have some familiarity with the term *industrial revolution* perhaps through television programmes of one sort or another or from memories of school history lessons. Whether this will continue into the future remains in doubt given the more recent government-encouraged trend for schools to return to the 'kings and queens' history teaching of an earlier era. The term refers to a crucial period of historical change with effects that were permanent and profound. The process of industrialisation involved a change in the way things were made. A predominantly agricultural economy gave way to a predominantly industrial one. Handicraft production carried out in people's homes or domestic workshops was replaced by production in factories. New business methods were developed and new systems of communications emerged[12].

Before the industrial revolution, most people worked on the land. Typically, family members co-operated in their activities and spent most of their time together. The sharp dividing line between work and leisure – or between work and 'life' – which most people in modern society experience, did not necessarily exist. Tasks, and the time they took, were dictated by the seasons and by the requirements of day-to-day farming. For most people, any scope for what we now call leisure would be built into and around the normal round of chores associated with daily survival.

> '*Social intercourse and labour are intermingled – the working day lengthens or contracts according to the task – and there is no great sense of conflict between labour and "passing the time of day"*'[13]

The growth of the factory system also typically involved a divorce between place of residence and place of work. Home and work became separated not only in and by time but also by place. For most people today 'work' is somewhere we travel to. Production and consumption – so closely combined in the pre-industrial rural economy – are split, with the family now associated directly only with the latter (spending the wage received for engaging in the production process). Industrialisation greatly accelerated the production of commodities and thereby the growth of a market economy. A system of production based primarily on immediate consumption (producing what you need – food, clothes, and so on – rather than to sell on) is replaced by one in which things are produced for exchange. Production for one's own family use largely disappears.

Before the revolution, people were often engaged in handicraft production which involved the production of single objects produced by one person or family group. Industrialisation changed this. The development of a factory system divided the process of production into increasingly smaller and separate tasks requiring the organisation and co-operation of large numbers of workers under one roof. The basic hand tools and craftsmanship of traditional methods of production were replaced by the growing use of machinery. With mechanisation the volume of produced items increased exponentially.

This growth of technology altered the relationship between the worker and what he or she produced. With traditional craftsmanship, the worker as producer had a large measure of control over their work. Take the making of a piece of furniture such as a chair. The craftsman would select the appropriate raw material (choice of suitable type and condition of wood), prepare it (cutting, sawing, planing, turning, shaping) and assemble it (using appropriate and well-practised joints the techniques of which would have been passed on through previous generations of craftsmen). With mechanisation and a factory system of producing furniture, the work for each of these tasks would be allotted to different groups of workers none of whom would ever need or even care to see the finished product. It is not difficult to see how the pride and sense of achievement of producing your own chair in your own time to your own design (and possibly even for your own use) is replaced by the alienating drudgery of labouring at the same task, performed repeatedly every few seconds or minutes, at a speed and form dictated by an overseer or even a machine, and which forms just one small part of the process of producing hundreds or thousands of exactly the same type of chair to be sat in by hundreds or thousands of anonymous backsides.

The industrial revolution took control away from the individual producer and placed it in the hands of the factory owner-manager. The simple co-operation of family members was replaced by the detailed regulation and control of large numbers of factory workers. As the factories got larger and their organisational structures more complex, the control function itself would be subject to a division of responsibility (among various types and levels of hierarchical management)[14]. In the 20th century, parallel developments in the production process would see the division of labour taken to new levels with the assembly line (and, eventually, automation would throw a whole new spanner into the works).

All this is good for the economy, we would be told today. And, on the face of it, it appeared to be good for the country at the time. The industrial revolution made Britain the wealthiest and most powerful nation on earth. It was certainly good for the profit margins of the industrial revolution's early generations of factory magnates. Whether it was also good for the workers is less obvious. Historians have long debated whether the mass of the population was better or worse off because of the industrial revolution. Although they have tried, it is a question that cannot be answered in any measurable sense precisely because of the massive transformation in society that the revolution brought about. As old ways of life disappear and new needs are created, it becomes impossible to compare like with like. Even on a narrow range of factors – wage levels, for example, or food prices – comparison pre- and post-industrialisation is meaningless if many people had previously produced much of their own food, with no cash exchange involved. As the sociologist Peter Townsend was fond of pointing out when discussing poverty, you cannot objectively assess today's poverty by yesterday's standards[15]. What is more to the point when attempting to compare standards of living before and during industrialisation, however, is the perception of those around at the time. And there is much evidence that many people did feel worse off, particularly if social as well as material factors are taken into account[16].

And one of the major social consequences of the industrial revolution – because it affected so many facets of people's lives – was urbanisation. Of course, urban living in the form of cities and towns pre-dated the revolution: it has existed for thousands of years. But the rapid growth of urban areas, and the movement of large numbers of people from rural areas to towns, does seem inevitably to follow industrialisation wherever the latter occurs. If a society is defined as urban once more than 50% of its population lives in towns and cities, then Britain officially became an urban society mid-way through the 19th century. New towns sprung up in the heart of the areas where the industrial revolution began: notably the textile towns of Lancashire. Existing cities expanded rapidly if they, too, were geographically favourable to the new industries. The population of London, for example, more than doubled in the first 40 years of the 1800s, while Manchester's tripled[17].

The rapid and uncontrolled expansion of urban areas gave rise to a panoply of factors all having a bearing on people's standard of living and how this was experienced: rising crime, disease, pollution, low life expectancy, poor and overcrowded housing (see Chapter 1) being some of the chief ones. The detail of some of the social and economic consequences of the industrial revolution – and of its corollary, urbanisation – moulded the lives of successive generations of Sprostons. They are evident at various stages in the rest of this book.

In addition to the central place devoted to the application of steam power, old school history books were apt to explain the industrial revolution as a series of apparently coincidental mechanical inventions that Britain had the good fortune, or expertise, to create at the right time: Kay's Flying Shuttle in 1733, Hargreaves's Spinning Jenny, 1767, Arkwright's Water Frame, 1769, Crompton's Mule, 1777. Undoubtedly, such developments and inventions were an essential part of the process, and the marrying of steam power to the factory organisation of production in the decades following the 1780s took industrialisation to a new level. But inventions do not by themselves become innovations. Just as it is no coincidence today that it is the computer and associated micro-technologies that display the most rapid change and make the greatest advances, it is not surprising that 250 years ago it was the textile industries. Technological innovations follow the money and the scent of more money: funds for Research and Development are far more forthcoming in those branches of industry that are already highly profitable.

In any case, the changes that occurred in Britain in the 18th and 19th centuries amounted to far more than a series of technical developments in the way things were produced. The industrial revolution involved, and followed from, major transformations in the way the economy and society was organised. It was also a period of rapid and fundamental social change that had major social consequences. Yet the term 'industrial revolution' was not used in Britain at the time (it is easier to recognise and to label periods of history with hindsight than when they are still taking place). French authors have been credited with the first uses of the term and Engels employed it directly in *The Condition of the Working Class in England*, published in Germany in 1845[18]. The first English translation of Engels's work did not appear until over 40 years later, however. By this time, the historian Arnold Toynbee had already published his best-selling *Lectures on the Industrial Revolution* and the term was being more generally used in this country[19].

The label, however, is not an uncontested one. 'Revolution' implies total and sudden change. While it certainly captures the all-embracing nature of the changes that were taking place, a period of a hundred years might not be regarded as sufficiently abrupt to be described as sudden. For this reason, the more neutral term 'industrialisation' is sometimes preferred as it denotes a process taking place over a period of time. It also allows a recognition that the changes did not suddenly get underway on 1st January 1750 nor end without warning on 31st December 1850. Not only are the ramifications of industrialisation still felt today, but developments linked to the process began earlier than the mid-18th century.

The great changes that became known as the industrial revolution did not appear as a bolt out of the blue. Industrialisation did not spring up from a historic clean sheet; there was a basis of industry going back, in some cases, for centuries. Locally, there is evidence suggesting that a glassworks had been operating between Rugeley and nearby Abbots Bromley from at least the first half of the 14th century[20], and from the even closer manor of Wolseley early in the following century[21]. Coal mining on Cannock Chase has been traced back as far as the 13th century, and the first blast furnace in the Midlands, which fundamentally altered the process of iron production, was built there in the 1560s[22]. Sixty years later the Chase also became the site for one of the earliest slitting mills (Slitting Mill is now the name of a small village a couple of miles south of Little Haywood), which provided cut iron rods for Staffordshire's already established nail industry[23].

But beyond the purely technical advances, one of the major developments which made the industrial revolution possible, and which started much earlier and developed more gradually, was a fundamental transformation of property relations. Landed property, supported by the old feudal relationships of lord and serf and by the traditional institutions of church and state, had been declining in importance since the late 14th and the 15th centuries.

Feudalism was both an economic and a social system. Economically based on the ownership of land, it was characterised by a pyramidal system of social stratification of broad classes, or 'estates', and involved reciprocal, but very unequal, rights and duties. Having already been established for some time in other parts of Europe, the feudal system was imposed on England following the Norman Conquest in 1066. The monarch granted land to feudal lords and to the relatively less powerful vassals or knights in return for military service. Further down the pyramid were freemen and yeomen with various grades of peasants or serfs at the base[24]. The peasants worked the land and in a predominantly agricultural society were therefore the economically productive class who provided the means of subsistence for everyone. As part of the feudal deal, they were required to hand over a proportion of their produce, or to devote a proportion of their labour time, to the local lord of the manor. They would also be expected to fight and die in wars if called upon by their feudal superiors to whom everyone was bound to be loyal (as well as owing allegiance to the monarch). In return, serfs typically held a small piece of land on which to grow food for their families[25] and were permitted to graze their livestock on common land. Legally, they were tied to the land of the place where they were born, not being allowed to leave without permission[26].

As far as the peasantry was concerned, the duties were therefore many and onerous and the rights few and far between. But, as with most enduring systems of social inequality, feudalism was reinforced by a religious ideology. Through the institution of the church, inequalities were justified as being the will of God. This is well expressed in the verse, often omitted when sung today, from the Victorian hymn *All Things Bright and Beautiful:*

'The rich man at his castle,
The poor man at his gate.
God made them high or lowly,
And ordered their estate.'

The fact that such lines could be penned at a time when most of the economic relationships of feudalism had been long dead, nonetheless shows the more enduring social and cultural trappings of the system.

A combination of factors led to the decline of feudalism and made way for the eventual emergence of a different type of economic system as the dominant form. They included the growth of towns, an increase in domestic and international trade, the greater use of money as a means of exchange, the development of the nation state (and a more centralised form of government), and the gradual replacement of the direct labour service of serfdom by various grades and classes of free peasants, yeoman and rent-paying tenants[27]. Following the Civil War half way through the 17th century, modern freehold had finally replaced feudal tenures. This effectively converted the English landed classes from feudal lords into land owners who could now *'do what they liked with their land'*[28]. But, over the longer period, the emergence of a greater number of free, but landless, peasants had also been in part due to the willingness of sections of the peasantry to fight against the economic and social positions which feudalism had imposed on them. Notable among this resistance was the Peasants' Revolt of 1381. Although at the time the revolt was ruthlessly dealt with and hundreds of peasants executed, its role in helping to accelerate feudalism's decline has since been recognised.

By the 17th century, a commodity-producing money economy and wage-labour were becoming dominant, reflecting a transition from a feudal to a capitalist economy. Through the 'putting-out' system, merchants were taking possession of the production process which was becoming more centralised. The putting-out system was an early form of subcontracting and its growth was an extension of the 'domestic system' or 'cottage industry' which had existed for centuries[29]. As the names imply, families would be working from home producing textile products, for example, or, more likely working on one stage in the production of a textile product – such as spinning or weaving. The raw materials would be brought to them by merchants who would later collect the finished, or part-finished, articles in order to sell them or take them to other homes for the next stage of the manufacturing process.

Rather than buying the products from the home workers, the merchants increasingly came to own the materials and often the equipment (the home spinning and weaving machines, for example) as well, paying the home workers only for their labour. For some merchants, this practice grew into large enterprises, renting out machinery *'sometimes to many hundreds of dependent families'*[30]. These merchants, then, were the early capitalists. Significant changes were taking place on the land, too, where it became cheaper to rear sheep (to meet the growing demand for wool), rather than to continue to house and provide work for people to cultivate it. Families who had worked the land for generations were being evicted.

The economic and social changes that led eventually to the industrial revolution therefore go much further back in time and it was to be a long while before industrial capital began to dominate the economy. Capital is wealth that is used to make more wealth. You may prefer to keep your savings under the mattress for a rainy day or to prevent the bankers from using it to pay themselves fat bonuses. But mattress money will fall in value if prices increase (which they have a nasty habit of doing). It certainly won't produce any additional money for you in the future. Some sort of investment is normally required for money to make more money. For many decades before the period of the industrial revolution, some people with money to spare had begun to invest quite heavily in those sectors of the economy – including, but not only, agriculture – that seemed to offer the chance of a good return.

The early investors often came from the growing bands of merchants. Some had made their fortune from the international slave trade which played a significant role in this country's economic expansion. In addition to bankrolling some of the agricultural developments of the 18th century, the slave trade was also chiefly responsible for building up the wealth of the ports of Bristol and

Liverpool, as well as augmenting that of London. Other sources of capital investment were found among those from the landed classes in search of new ways of protecting their estates and multiplying their inherited wealth. For motives or reasons that are still debated by historians[31], these individuals, rather than spend all their profits on luxuries and riotous living, would habitually reinvest all or most of their returns in the same or other ventures and continue to do so. This continual investment and reinvestment became quite fashionable. Most industry that existed in the pre-factory days was relatively small scale and often localised: rurally-based domestic textile and clothes-making concerns, iron manufacture and the extractive industries (coal, lead and tin mining, for example). It was these sorts of enterprises that often attracted the voguish investor, but only if ways could be found of extending their reach, geographically and economically, beyond the merely local. And as these ways (primarily forms of transport and communications) themselves would require considerable amounts of capital investment, they too provided outlets for aspiring capitalists. Capital began to accumulate.

These changes in the basis of property relations and forms of capital investment and capital accumulation did not, of course, happen overnight. Furthermore, the old social and class divisions of feudalism continued in quite visible ways in the countryside. An elderly local resident, reflecting on life in the villages in the first half of the 20th century, remarked:

'[T]here was a distinct difference in social classes. Everyone knew their place. People living in Colwich and Little Haywood lacked the paternalism of Shugborough ... and were seemingly more independent... [Yet] non-attendees [at church] had to explain themselves to the lord of the manor rather than the priest.'[32]

The historian Harold Perkin points to the two faces of this paternalism. Loyalty and obedience, in the form of cap-doffing servility and doing as you are told, would be rewarded. Disloyalty and insubordination would be punished[33]. Admittedly, the range of rewards and punishments had somewhat diminished by the 20th century. But the social control of a village, where everyone knew everyone else and what they were up to, and the control over employment that the local wealthy and landed classes could exert, were still powerful tools. This does not mean that everyone willingly accepted the consequences of such an unbalanced and, to today's eyes, patently unfair system. Running all along the north-eastern edge of Lord Lichfield's Shugborough estate, from Great Haywood to Little Haywood, is a high brick wall. On sunny days it casts a near-permanent shadow over the single pavement and much of the roadway. The existence of this wall has always been contentious locally. Until quite recently there were residents of the villages who maintained it should never have been built as it cut off access to common land. Indeed the initial construction of the wall was frequently delayed by irate locals tearing down newly built sections overnight[34].

Remnants of the feudal system can still be seen in various national and local institutions, customs and practices: the monarchy, the honours system, the old universities, the surviving forms of social distinctions in English village life, the concentration of land ownership, the cultural concerns with detailed status signifiers, the appeal of TV series such as Downton Abbey ….the list could continue. They certainly had not died out in Little Haywood at the time of William's death in 1896. The farm and the Navigation Inn, which doubled as the farmhouse, did not form part of his estate on his death. William had been a tenant farmer renting the fields and the Inn from their owner, the third Earl of Lichfield who owned much of the land surrounding Shugborough Hall, the family seat next to Great Haywood. Although no longer a feudal relationship in an economic sense, renting farmland from your local aristocrat would not release you from the social obligations that still prevailed. The relationship was hardly one of equality between two business partners. Farm tenancies would come up for renewal very regularly, often on a yearly basis, emphasising the dependency of the tenant farmer on the landowner. In turn, this would also mean insecure employment prospects for any farm workers who might be hired by the tenant farmer.

The uncertainties associated with tenant farming could well explain why William embraced multiple business interests. After his sudden departure from this world, Elizabeth and the family were therefore faced with urgent decisions about the future of the businesses he had left behind. Elizabeth also had to consider what to do with the cash her husband had left in his will. Would she blow it all on a luxury, no-expense spared continental holiday, or just a bit of it on a few weeks in Bognor? Perhaps she might splash out on a state-of-the-art replacement horse-powered carriage – with replacement pony, if necessary – or even one of the new motorised models? With no birth-children of her own, would she be prepared to help out her many surviving step-children – and, if so, all of them or only some? More sensibly if mundanely, in the days before the introduction of state pensions, would she invest it for her old age or even to provide an immediate and regular income? Given the typical returns on investments at the time, the sum left by William could have produced an annual income considerably more than that enjoyed by many of her fellow villagers.

Chapter 4

To the Village by Water... and Christopher

At the time of his death, ten of William's seventeen children were still living: six sons and four daughters. All the daughters were married by this time and all had children of their own: more than 20 in total (with more to follow). The sons had been rather less prolific with not quite half that number by the Spring of 1896; their most (re)productive years still lay ahead. Eventually, there would be at least 55 grandchildren (including Nel): quite impressive, but a long way behind the fecundity of William and Elizabeth 1.

Three of the daughters and one of the sons had moved away from the village. The decisions to be made about William's bequests would be of particular interest to the six children still living in Little Haywood or Colwich. It appears that, at least for a while, Elizabeth herself ran a farm business but not from the Navigation Inn. Soon after her husband's death she returned to live and work at the nearby grocery shop which her family had kept on after her marriage[1]. By 1900 she is also recorded as the village post-mistress. She shared the house with stepson Albert who is also listed as a farmer, on a self-employed basis[2].

In the years immediately before William's death, the eldest surviving son, James, had worked as farm bailiff on a neighbouring 200-acre farm which his father also tenanted from Lord Lichfield[3]. This was Haywood Park Farm and James had been living at the farmhouse there with his young family. After William died, however, the tenancy of Haywood Park ended and James moved back into Navigation Inn. As well as taking over from his father as publican, he also ran the farm and the coal business, initially in partnership with two of his brothers: Herbert and the youngest, William[4].

Mira, the oldest surviving child of William and Elizabeth 1, had eleven children and was living in Colwich with her husband, a self-employed bricklayer. The only brother to have left the village,

Henry, was already continuing in one of his father's footsteps having set up a coal merchant's business in the market town of Stone[5].

This leaves Nel's father, Christopher. Aged 32 when his father died, Christopher was well-known in the village and popular within his community. Two years earlier, when the first elections were held for the newly established Colwich Parish Council, Christopher had topped the poll. Born in 1863, Christopher was the fourteenth child of William and Elizabeth 1 and the first to be born in Little Haywood. As with his brothers and sisters, but unlike his father, he received some years of formal education at the local school. By the time of his father's death, Christopher was already a farmer but either he was not invited to join his brothers' business in running Navigation Farm or he chose not to. He perhaps preferred to continue farming the land adjacent to where he lived on the other side of the village and to carry out his duties as parish councillor.

It would seem, then, that a part of William's legacy may have been used to further Elizabeth's own business activities and possibly also those of some of her stepchildren. At the least the money would have facilitated the business and living rearrangements that would have been required. She went on to outlive her husband by 26 years but still held a substantial slice of the inheritance when she died. Either she spent little of the money during her lifetime or she continued to prosper financially (or some combination of both). In the meantime, Navigation farm and inn remained with the family and the second-generation Sproston presence in the local community continued and seemed secure.

Unlike some of the towns and villages in the north and in the south of the county, industrialisation did not transform Little Haywood and its close neighbours into a seething hub of factories, smokestacks, warehouses and intensely concentrated back-to-back housing. They were however directly affected by the new systems of communications and transport that were also a fundamental part of the industrial revolution. These new systems have left clearly visible marks on the topography of the villages and in many ways they still define and pattern the lives of those living there today.

One development in transport in particular also explains the course of the Sproston history. From old Job Sproston, via the move of his son Thomas and grandson William from Cheshire to Staffordshire, through to great-grandson Christopher, this development was crucial. Christopher was the first member of the family to be born at the Navigation Inn and therein lies the clue. Since *navigation* is an early name for canal, pubs with that name are typically found at canal-sides.

Canals were not an invention of the industrial revolution. The history of canal construction for transport purposes can be traced to at least as far back as the 6th century BC with the building of a link between Egypt's River Nile and the Red Sea[6]. The Chinese were also great early canal builders, culminating in the Grand Canal in the 7th century AD, and, later, credited with the invention of a type of lock still used in canals today[7]. Although the Romans built artificial navigable waterways, such as the Foss Dyke in England[8], the earliest European canal is said to be that constructed in Italy between 1179 and 1209 to transport marble for the building of the cathedral in Milan[9]. Almost a century earlier, however – and for a similar purpose, though admittedly on a much smaller scale – a short canal had been dug in the east of England. From the River Wensum, this canal was used to carry, over the final few hundred yards of its journey, the caen stone from Normandy which was used to build Norwich Cathedral[10]. Canals were also constructed on occasions to bypass unnavigable sections of rivers, an early example being the short Exeter Canal in the 16th century. But apart from these, the first canal proper to be opened in the British Isles was Ireland's 35-mile long Newry Canal in 1742[11].

So, as with the process of industrialisation itself, *'the canal age did not spring suddenly to life in the 1750s'*[12]. In England, attempts to make rivers more navigable had been increasing over the previous century and included artificial cuts and by-pass locks[13]. Such improvements were seen as important for trade because, with nowhere being more than 70 crow-flying miles from the sea, navigable waterways could often penetrate into the heart of the country and provide access to the coastal ports.

An increasing demand from Cheshire salt manufacturers for the cheaper transport of coal from the Warrington area, led to the opening of England's first industrial canal – the Sankey or St Helens

Canal – in 1757[14]. This pre-dates by four years the Bridgewater Canal which history books are fond of claiming as the first of the canal age. The fame of the latter was perhaps in part due to the publicity surrounding its opening and to some stunning features including an aqueduct and a tunnel[15]. Later, it was because of the strategic importance of the canal in the rapid expansion of Manchester as the predominant industrial and commercial centre. The canal was named after the third Duke of Bridgewater, Francis Egerton, who commissioned its construction. It was common practice for the sons of aristocratic families to embark on a Grand Tour of Europe, a sort of early version of the gap-year, and it was during his tour that the young Egerton was impressed by some of the European canals he had seen. He engaged the engineer James Brindley to build a waterway that would carry coal from the Duke's mines at Worsley to Manchester. Up to the building of the canal, there had been little economic incentive to exploit the coal reserves because of the high costs of carrying the coal to where it would be needed.

The Bridgewater Canal was a huge success. The price of coal in Manchester halved[16]. His coal was in great demand. The Duke became very rich. He was no doubt also seen as a role model by would-be investors, and willing investors were not in short supply. With the fashion for re-investing profits in order to make even bigger profits becoming well established, the owners of, and investors in, the textile mills, the coal mines, the potteries inevitably focused on the 'how' questions: how to increase production and how to sell the products more widely. A key element in the answers to these questions was transport – the transport of raw materials to the factories and the transport of finished goods to the markets. Some of the interest came from the Lancashire textile merchants wanting to ship their goods between Manchester and the port of Liverpool, for example. But it was for heavy and bulky materials, especially, where transport costs had to be low, where much of the demand lay. Many of the materials needed in abundance for industrialisation – brick, stone, ores, timber and, in particular, coal – were bulky. The previous modes of available transport, mainly horse-drawn conveyances along poorly maintained tracks and roadways, were too costly to move these types of goods over other than very short distances[17]. As a consequence, quarries, mines and related manufacturing units tended to remain localised in scope and static in size. The promise of canals was to change this picture by slashing transport costs and allowing markets to expand geographically. The Bridgewater and Sankey Canals showed this could be done.

The vast majority of capital for canal building was raised privately. Acts of Parliament were required to sanction particular projects and the government would sometimes use these to encourage the construction of specific canals. And after the passing of the Poor Employment Act in 1817 a small amount of public money was made available as loans for public works, which could include canal building. The take-up, however, was hardly overwhelming; not much interest was shown[18]. Apart from these initiatives, there was little in the way of state intervention or public funding.

But with a prevailing investment climate of optimism, further encouraged by low interest rates, private capital was not hard to come by. As well as the keen interest shown by merchants and industrialists, there were also those in the landed classes who were persuaded of the lucrative possibilities of the canal. Canals, they thought, would increase the capital or rental values of their estates. Even more financially rewarding, a canal could make viable the previously uneconomic extraction of any minerals beneath their land[19]. The Duke of Bridgewater's experience is, and was, the obvious example. It was through this type of investment channel that some of the excess profits – accrued from the increases in agricultural yields and rents since the mid-eighteenth century – were used to help finance the canal boom[20].

And, for quite a lengthy period, a 'boom' it was. From the 1770s, there was an enormous amount of canal building. England's major industrial centres and navigable rivers began to be connected by trunk-line canals to form a revolutionary new communications system. The River Mersey was linked to the River Severn, the Severn to the Thames and the Mersey to the Trent and to the Thames. These links were significant because an island economy cannot properly grow without internal transport connections to its ports, for access to export markets. By 1790, this frenetic era of canal construction meant that all the major ports – Liverpool (crucial to the Lancashire textile industry), Bristol, London and Hull (providing a further boost to the Yorkshire woollen industry[21]) – were connected. Further, the hub of the network was at the 'Grand Cross' formed by Birmingham, Coventry and Great Haywood in the Midlands, thereby allowing subsequent industrialisation to be driven by the industrial powerhouse of Birmingham and the Black Country. According to Peter Mathias, developing the local canal system of the Cross was

'the most important single step in opening up the central industrial region and the Midland coalfield to the major ports on all sides of the island'[22].

The connection to London from the Midlands and the north-west was strengthened in 1805 with the opening of the Grand Junction Canal. This provided a direct link to the capital whereas previously only a narrow canal joined Coventry to the Thames at Oxford[23].

It is no surprise that Birmingham's business community became involved in canal investment. It prospered and the town (city status was still a century away) expanded very quickly: by the end of the 1700s, its population was almost five times as high as it had been a century earlier. Although living conditions in general improved somewhat during the second half of the 19th century, the working population of Birmingham did not escape all the attendant social problems that rapid, unchecked and unplanned industrialisation brings in its wake – poor housing, ill health, disease, poverty[24].

By the beginning of 19th century, then, the industrial revolution was well underway and had been for some time. The canals were playing an essential role as they had become a key part of Britain's industrial infrastructure. The canal network was providing access to markets previously unattainable and was freeing up resources hitherto uneconomic to exploit. Coal was the outstanding example. Most of the country's raw materials were put to use domestically, fuelling the apparently insatiable needs of the manufacturing industries – and this, of course, included coal. Additionally, though, coal had become sufficiently available to become an important export, too – thanks to the canal network and its links to the ports.

But canals were also stimulating the economy in other ways. They provided employment for thousands of workers. Large 'navvy' (inland navigation) gangs were required to dig out the canals, carve out tunnels and build bridges. The navvies were the real builders of the canals. Engineers such as James Brindley deservedly receive recognition for their vision and their design skills, but it was the navvies who laboured hard and long in all weathers to convert their plans into reality. Later navvies were recruited from Scotland and Ireland, as well as the north and midlands of England, but initially they were more likely to be local farm workers[25].

'Navvies were men of legend… Working conditions on site were harsh and dangerous and many navvies were killed or injured. Tunnelling was particularly hazardous. The navvies' living accommodation was primitive; perhaps just makeshift turf hovels. The truck system (where food and other necessities were bought from the contractor) was rife.'[26]

Other jobs needed to be filled. Boats needed to be built. Once up and running, the canals as well as the canal architecture and the boats had to be maintained, as did the locks. The boats had to be operated. Canals had become a major job creation scheme in their own right. And jobs delivered wages which provided purchasing power which in itself boosted the economy.

There were downsides, as well. Some localised sectors of the economy, often involving handicraft production, had previously been protected from competition by high transport costs. With the advent of the canals, they lost their monopoly position. They would go to the wall, with all the consequent personal hardships and social disruption that a pre-welfare state society in a state of flux can produce. Things did not always work out well for investors, either. As with the dot-com bubble of the 1990s, there were some silly speculative investments as over-enthusiastic punters got caught up in the canal boom. These often involved uneconomic canals constructed in agricultural districts[27].

Nonetheless, one of the enduring effects of the canal era was the creation of large conurbations – Merseyside, Manchester,

London and, of course, the West Midlands which emerged as the central region of the network. And within that region, 'Staffordshire ... became the hub of the national canal system'[28]. This was largely due to the construction of one canal in particular. And it is this canal which explains not only the route of the Sproston journey but also the reasons for it. Hassall Green, Rode Heath, Church Lawton, Weston-upon-Trent, Shirleywich, Colwich and Great Haywood all feature in the story of the Sproston family's inter-generational journey from its starting point in Middlewich to its end point at Little Haywood. All these places lie along the Trent and Mersey Canal.

Because it was a key part of James Brindley's vision to connect England's major rivers, the Trent & Mersey was initially known as the Grand Trunk Canal. At its north end, the canal links to the River Mersey by the Bridgewater Canal which it joins at Preston Brook. It cuts south-easterly through Cheshire and then Staffordshire where it eventually switches north-easterly, ending to the east of Shardlow by joining the River Trent at the Derbyshire-Leicestershire boundary. There are intersections with other canals at Great Haywood and at Fradley to form the 'Grand Cross' of waterways connecting the Humber, Mersey, Thames and Severn estuaries[29].

A significant early step in the Trent & Mersey project took place very close to Little Haywood and Colwich in December, 1765. To galvanise interest in and funding for the venture, a meeting of 'the Company of Proprietors of the Navigation from the Trent to the Mersey' was held at the adjacent village of Wolseley Bridge. Notable attendees were the pottery manufacturer Josiah Wedgwood, canal investors' darling the Duke of Bridgewater, Thomas Anson, the owner of the local Shugborough estate, and the industrialist Matthew Boulton of Smethwick, later to find fame – with James Watt – for the building of steam engines. Many other local landowners, merchants and manufacturers were also invited[30]. Events then moved rapidly and the development of the Trent & Mersey Canal was given the go-ahead by an Act of Parliament in 1766.

Eleven years later the entire length of the canal was in operation, although the first long, eastern and southern, section as far as

Shugborough had opened as early as 1770[31]. The inaugural spadeful of soil had been dug out by Josiah Wedgwood[32] who was a principal investor in the canal. He saw the potential for cutting the cost of transporting the required bulky raw materials and for a smoother and safer carriage of his finished products to the ports for world-wide export. The pottery industry of north Staffordshire, of which Wedgwood's wares would become the best known, was the big mover behind the Trent & Mersey. Before it was built, Cornwall clay and Sussex flint had to be shipped to north Cheshire and taken from the port of Runcorn by horse pack on rutted and pot-holed roads to the potteries of Stoke-on-Trent[33]. This was costly and slow, but even worse was the need to transport the delicate china and earthenware products by the same means. Even though, on Wedgwood's initiative, improvements to the road from his factory had been undertaken which linked the Potteries to the national road network[34], a more suitable alternative was needed. Confident that the new waterway would deliver the goods, Wedgwood had a new factory built next to it at Etruria shortly after work on the canal started. Many other factory owners followed suit as potteries sprung up along nearby sections of the canal[35]. The Wedgwood pottery empire became one of the largest and well-known manufacturers of tableware in the world[36] and remained so for 250 years. Following years of decline, a series of takeovers and buy-outs and the shifting of much of the manufacturing base overseas, however, the making of Wedgwood products in the UK is now severely reduced[37].

For the first century of the Trent & Mersey's operation, transport delays occurred because of the need to transfer cargoes to the canal from the River Weaver 50 feet below. The clay destined for the Potteries, for example, which had been carried by coastal shipping from Cornwall to Runcorn on the River Mersey, had to be unloaded from vessels on the Weaver and reloaded onto canal boats on the Trent & Mersey. As a small island, Britain does lend itself to water transport. The downside is that it is also quite hilly in places and water does not flow uphill. In many places, therefore, devices were needed to remedy this deficiency. Tunnels are one possibility and another, the lock, became a common method. Far more rare is the boat lift such as the gigantic Anderton Lift, near Northwich in Cheshire. Built in 1875, it was to become one of two celebrated feats of engineering along the Trent & Mersey canal. Designer Edwin Clark's revolutionary solution to the height disparity was the world's first hydraulically operated system to raise the boats without the need to unload[38]. Originally steam-powered, the lift now operates electrically and has become a participatory tourist attraction[39].

A few miles farther on, the canal reaches the historically and strategically important town of Middlewich, the spiritual home of the Sproston diaspora. Sited at the confluence of three rivers, the town was also a junction of seven major Roman roads. For the Romans in Britain and later Sprostons alike, therefore, perhaps all roads lead to Middlewich, rather than to Rome. But canals eventually were to put their stamp on the place, too. Physically and economically built on salt, the Romans called the town Salinae and salt extraction has been a main industry since those times[40]. Before the development of more modern methods, salt was used to preserve food and was thus in great demand[41]. Today, more than half the cooking salt used in the UK is produced at the British Salt factory on the banks of the Trent & Mersey canal in Middlewich[42]. The need to distribute the product to its markets, and the inward transport of coal from North Staffordshire for use in its manufacture, made Middlewich an important user of the canal system. In addition to the Trent & Mersey, the Shropshire Union Canal – linking parts of the West Midlands canal system to the Manchester Ship Canal – passes through the town.

Leaving Middlewich, as at some stage in his earlier life did Job Sproston, the Trent & Mersey begins an ascent through a series of locks. The long upwards haul (which at one time was known as Heartbreak Hill) continues to Harecastle Hill, taking in Hassall Green, Rode Heath and Church Lawton[43]. Early in the journey, the canal passes close to, but not through, Sandbach, a market town famous for the production of heavy goods vehicles built by Foden and ERF (both companies are no longer there[44]) and, within footballing and Sproston circles, for being the birthplace of an England international full-back who played alongside the legendary Stanley Matthews. Some towns may have grander claims to fame, but Bert Sproston deserves a mention for his considered assessment of Adolf Hitler before the outbreak of the Second World War. During an England team trip to Berlin for an international match with Germany in May 1938, Bert turned to Stanley and said:

> *"I know nowt 'bout politics and t'like. All I knows is football. But t'way I see it, yon 'Itler fella is an evil little twat."*[45]

Seventy-four years later, another England international full-back was reprimanded for tweeting the same noun in comments about the English Football Association. Bert Sproston's opinion of the German Chancellor is, of course, far more excusable since it has the justifiable defence of being true.

Sandbach parish is the district of Cheshire where Job Sproston married Mary Condliffe in early 1786[46]. Job was 22, his wife one year older, and the first of their five children was baptised less than seven weeks later. All their children were born or baptised in the area, with Odd Rode being more specifically recorded as the birthplace of the youngest. The Odd Rode/Rode Heath district is by the Trent & Mersey and it was Job who started the family connection with the canal that was to last through four generations and be responsible for the direction of the family's future. There is a suggestion that Mary's family, from nearby Betchton, may have possessed some wealth through land ownership[47]. Mary's great-great-great-grandfather, John Condliffe, had married into the prosperous and influential landowning Brough/Burgh family from North Staffordshire. It seems, however, that most of the family wealth passed to John's wife's brother[48]. Nonetheless, if any of it had trickled down through the subsequent generations of Condliffes it could have been used to help Job in setting up in business as a boat builder. He was certainly in the right place at the right time to take advantage of the burgeoning demand for narrow boats on the busy Trent & Mersey Canal.

Did financial success in his boatbuilding career help him to obtain legal advice which allowed him to live thirteen years longer than might have been the case? This is speculation, but it is known that, in September 1809, Job Sproston, boat builder of Odd

Rode, was committed to gaol charged with "killing and slaying" Samuel Bostock, also of Odd Rode. Eight months later, however, in a teasingly brief reference to the trial at Chester Assizes, the *Manchester Mercury* reported that there was insufficient evidence to proceed with the case[49]. And that is all that is now known of the Odd Rode murder mystery. Job's life eventually ended in 1823 in nearby Hassall Green. It was here he had his boatbuilding premises, possibly sited by Lock 57 where, today, the old canal-side buildings house a café/restaurant and shop which cater for the passing canal leisure trade. At Hassall Green, the tranquillity often associated with small village life is now disturbed by the stilted M6 motorway which towers and roars overhead, an unavoidable visible and audible presence which casts a permanent shadow on the few houses beneath.

Thomas, the eldest son of Job and Mary, followed his father as a boat builder but then worked the canals as a boatman. He married Ann Daines from the village of Astbury, only a few miles from where Thomas had grown up, and they went on to have 12 children, possibly more. Evidence from various stages of their lives suggests that the family, or most of the family, lived as well as worked on their boat. Living conditions on all canal boats were cramped but especially so on the narrowboats of the Trent & Mersey. The narrowness of the locks, and in places of the canal itself, restricted the boats to a maximum overall width of seven feet. Although they could be up to 72 feet long, most of the space was required for the cargo and cabins were tiny. Living space would have been even tighter for a family the size of Thomas and Ann's. Although it seems that their three daughters were brought up away from the canal, most likely by their maternal grandparents back in Astbury, the cabin would have been home to all the boys and their parents. The dimensions of a typical narrowboat cabin might be no more than 8 feet by 6.5 feet with a height of 5 feet (sometimes lower)[50]. As well as being the only place to store the entire range of their provisions, domestic utensils and personal belongings, the cabin would have to meet all the cooking, eating, sleeping and personal hygiene needs of the whole family. Some boats did have an additional cabin at the front but these were even smaller – allowing sleeping place for only one adult or two children – and some families worked two boats[51].

> *'Sanitation on the canals was extremely primitive… People just used a chamber pot, and tipped its contents over the side of the boat.'*

And, in a fashion familiar to non-motorway road-users today:

> *'Even as late as the twentieth century, few canal companies bothered to provide canal-side WCs for their workers. People hopped behind the nearest hedge for convenience, or resorted to the towpath if there was no cover.'*[52]

Fresh water was scarce and the insanitary conditions and extreme overcrowding on a family-operated boat made it a risky place for babies and young children in particular. The nature of the cargoes, which could include nightsoil and refuse transported from the towns, would encourage vermin[53] and leaks from chemicals and other volatile or dangerous substances presented further hazards. Mortality rates among boatpeople were far higher than for other outside workers. Deaths from drowning were not uncommon[54].

Most canal boatmen did not own the boats which they operated. Except for a relatively small number of owner/boaters, the boats typically belonged to the carrying company. Instead of a regular wage, a boatman was paid by the journey or cargo out of which he would pay his steerer and any additional crew plus the upkeep costs of his horse. It is the main reason why boaters worked long (14 or 15 hour) days, seven days a week, and often seemed to be in a hurry. Any delay would cost them dearly. It is also why it made economic sense to have your family on board – as your (unpaid) crew. In addition, if the family lived together on the boat, the expense of renting a house could be spared[55]. Many families, though, strove to keep a base on land, even if they did not live there a great deal[56]. In some cases it seems that the canal companies owned properties which bordered the canals. Some of these might have been rented by boatpeople but the type of accommodation was usually smaller and of poorer quality than that provided for lockkeepers, for example. In 1876 a factory inspector referred to some boatpeople who worked the Trent & Mersey Canal living in 'small houses and sheds'[57].

Despite the long hours and poor living conditions, it may be thought that the open-air life and freedom from the discipline and rigours of factory work afforded boatpeople with some advantages over the workers in the sprawling towns and cities of early industrial Britain. There might have been something in this argument when the weather was fair and the delays few. But in harsh winters, with constant exposure to driving winds, rain or snow and with the lack of income when severe frosts prevented travel, it would have been difficult to appreciate the comparison. Furthermore, conditions aboard canal boats remained largely unregulated and beyond the remit of government inspectors for far longer than workplaces in the towns.

Although theirs was a peripatetic existence, Thomas and Ann seem to have used the village, and civil parish, of Church Lawton as a base before their move to Staffordshire in the late 1820s. Lying on the Trent & Mersey canal, it is ten locks up, but only a few miles, from Hassall Green and so represents a further stage in the very gradual southwards migration of the Sprostons. To the north-west of Stoke-on-Trent, Church Lawton is situated between the towns of Alsager and Kidsgrove. As a result of ribbon development, today it appears as a continuation of both.

At least five of Thomas's older children were baptised in the village. All Saints Church was known as a boaters' church[58], indicating that canal boatpeople were something of a closed community. A theory that the first boatpeople were of Romany extraction has since been discredited and it is likely that they came from varied backgrounds and previous occupations[59]. Once established, however, boating families often inter-married and 'penetration by outsiders' was not encouraged[60]. Although such endogamous relationships did not apply to Thomas or his son William, the custom for boaters' children to follow the family occupation over generations did.

It is not surprising that boatpeople tended to seek their own company: it can be seen as a rational reaction to the low esteem in which they were held by others in society. In the 19th century, boatmen acquired a reputation for being thieving, fighting drunkards. 'A more lawless class of men do not exist than the canal boatmen' opined the Legal Observer in 1839[61], following reports of poaching, pilfering from cargoes, brawls with other boatmen and lockkeepers, and disorderly behaviour after bouts of heavy drinking.

The conviction in 1840 of three boatmen for the rape and murder of Christina Collins, a canal boat passenger, dragged down the general reputation of boatpeople even further[62]. As it was less expensive than stage coach, Christina had paid to travel from Lancashire to London by canal. Twice on the journey she had complained of the 'roughness and coarseness' of the crew which made her feel unsafe. Later she was seen between Great Haywood and Weston being attacked by three men attempting to force her into the cabin of a boat. Her body was found in the canal between Colwich and Rugeley[63].

Two of the convicted boatmen, who may well have been known to Thomas and his family, were publicly hanged before a large crowd outside Stafford prison; the third had his death sentence commuted to transportation for life at the last minute. The press coverage of the event and the court case not only condemned the three guilty men but also extended its disapproval to boatpeople as a group:

> 'The prisoners were rather rough looking men and their dress and appearance completely indicated the class to which they belonged...
> [Two of the men] confessed that their general habits had been of the most profligate and depraved character; though not differing much from those of the class of men to which they belonged. We understand it was painful to hear their account of the scenes which are of daily occurrence amongst boatmen. Thieving, it appears, is reckoned to be an accomplishment, and those men are sought the most, by the captains of the boats, who can pilfer the boats the most adroitley [sic] and to the greatest extent.'[64]

All this would have done little to endear boatpeople in general to the local communities in Colwich and the Haywoods. And once a group of people become recognised as outsiders, the stereotypes multiply – and this can apply to those who come to their defence as well as to those who condemn:

> *'The boatmen loved to sing and dance while they enjoyed their ale: "the big burly men are wonderfully light of foot, and keep time accurately"'*[65]

Unruly, beer-swilling thieves and ne'er-do-wells they may be, but they have a great sense of rhythm! As Sue Wilkes has recognised, however, in addition to offering overnight stabling for the horse, the canal-side pub would provide a convenient, recreational respite at the end of a long day:

> *'It must have been a relief to exchange the confined space of the cabin for a couple of hours in a warm, welcoming taproom'*[66]

One such place would have been the Navigation Inn at Little Haywood which would eventually be home to William and his large family. Its first clientele were the navvies who built the Trent & Mersey[67]. Once that stretch of the canal was opened it would be a place for a boatman to relax with other boatpeople, with those similarly viewed with suspicion or hostility by the communities they passed through. They would be recognisable as boaters – through their shared specialised vocabulary and, according to some writers, their distinctive clothing:

> *'Boatmen sported bright neckerchiefs and beautifully embroidered belts and braces… Boatwomen were warmly and practically dressed, with a full-length skirt, a blouse, a pinafore to keep them clean and a shawl. They wore bonnets profusely adorned with long, heavy frills, which helped keep the sun off their heads and necks… Men, women and children wore stout boots or clogs.'*[68]

While boatpeople may have formed *'a distinct group within the working class'*[69], there are doubts, though, about the extent of some of these alleged differences. The clothing, particularly of the women, would not have differed greatly from that worn by many other working class women in the 19th century, for example[70]. Nonetheless, boatpeople were subject to the effects of the prejudices and ignorance common among sections of the general population. The itinerancy of their occupation would mark them out as strangers in the communities they passed through and they could be abused or refused service in local shops, for example[71].

The stereotypes, press speculation and the general anti-boater climate of the period proved fertile ground for the moral crusaders so prevalent in Victorian society. The Mary Whitehouses and Melanie Phillipses of the day thought that the undesirable activities of boaters were due to *'their lack of moral and religious education'*[72]. There were renewed missionary campaigns designed to instil Christian values into the Godless boatmen and their families. These included the establishment of floating chapels, the opening of refreshment rooms as alternatives to the pub and the distribution of bibles[73] (which were no doubt much appreciated by the largely illiterate recipients – at least they could be used as additional fuel for the cabin stoves).

In common with other groups on the receiving end of social opprobrium, negative characteristics become attributed to the ostracised rather than to the ostracisers. And these can remain as memories long after the days in which they were prevalent have passed: *'[The] boatees (as they were referred to locally) did not welcome curiosity'* is one Haywood resident's more polite, if distinctly cool, recollection of the early decades of the 20th century[74].

Immediately from Church Lawton, still proceeding southwards, the canal enters Staffordshire. The locks continue in rapid succession as they approach Harecastle Hill in north of the county. This massive sandstone ridge above Stoke-on-Trent was to present Brindley with his biggest design problem of the entire route and his gangs of navvies with some of their most backbreaking labour. He decided a tunnel was the only solution but on a scale that had never before been attempted. The tunnel was almost 1.75 miles long. To cut down on costs, time and labour, the canal width was reduced to allow only a single passageway and there would be no towpath. The horses therefore had to be unhitched and led over the hill while the boatmen (sometimes with the aid of professional 'leggers'), lying on their backs, legged the boats through – an exhausting exercise which could take two hours[75].

The tunnel soon became a bottleneck with boats queuing at each end to await their turn through. Another engineer, Thomas Telford, was hired to build a parallel tunnel in the mid-1820s. Traffic was eased by using both tunnels to provide a two-directional passage through the hill. This was fine until eventually subsidence from coal-mining in the area forced the permanent closure of the first tunnel[76]. But at least Telford's tunnel, the one still in use today, did have a towpath (that is until subsidence in the second tunnel necessitated its eventual removal)[77].

The Harecastle Tunnel is deservedly recognised as a great engineering achievement perhaps rivalled only by the Anderton Lift, but the latter was constructed a century after Brindley's labours. And it was Brindley who had drawn the overall picture of the canal network in linking England's waterways and chief ports, so crucial to industrialisation and to the part played in it by the county of Staffordshire.

Staffordshire is a landlocked county and its rivers are not navigable[78] yet, with its Black Country to the south and its potteries to the north, it was home to some of the earliest developments of the industrial revolution. Some system of communications which would allow the transport of raw materials and the outward flow of finished products was therefore required. In the early years of the 18th century there had been an unsuccessful attempt to connect the Trent and Severn rivers through a combination of river improvement and canal building[79]. But it was the construction of the Trent & Mersey Canal that really opened things up and placed Staffordshire at the centre. It connected the county to the ports of Liverpool on the west coast and Hull on the east. A link to the other major western port, Bristol, had already been forged with the opening of Brindley's Staffordshire and Worcestershire Canal in 1772. This linked the River Severn at Stourport with the Trent & Mersey at Great Haywood. By 1790, with a connection to London, via canals and the Thames, starting at Fradley, the Staffordshire hub of a national canal system was complete[80]. The inter-connected network of inland waterways provided a significant economic stimulus to

Staffordshire's industries and mines as well as to the salt fields of Cheshire. The savings in transport costs exceeded expectations, reducing them to a quarter of what had been charged to carry goods and materials by road[81]. More than half of the entire 93-mile length of the Trent & Mersey Canal meanders its way through Staffordshire and some of the effects of its boost to the county's economy were noted by one impressed contemporary observer:

'In a few years after [the canal] was finished, I saw ...manufacturers arise in the most unthought of places, new buildings and new streets spring up in many parts of Staffordshire, where it passes; the poor are no longer starving ... and the rich grow steadily richer.'[82]

James Brindley did not live to see the completion – he died in 1772 – but his achievements in linking the country's principal coastal rivers, and thereby its major sea-ports, were later celebrated by the Victorian writer Thomas Carlyle:

'Brindley ... has chained the seas together; his ships do visibly float over valleys, invisibly through the hearts of mountains; the Mersey and the Thames, the Humber and the Severn have shaken hands'[83].

And in addition to the trunk canals, of course, others could be built to provide short-cuts and access to and from particular centres of industry. The first of these branch canals to be built in England was Brindley's Birmingham Canal, opening the year of his death and running through the Black Country between Birmingham and north-west of Wolverhampton[84].

Within a year or two of the opening of the second Harecastle Tunnel in 1827, Thomas and Ann Sproston, with most of their growing family (including a five or six year old William), would have emerged at the southern exit to continue their move to Staffordshire. Passing through the city of Stoke-on-Trent and the Wedgwood factory at Etruria, they would eventually arrive at Stone. The town had been chosen for the headquarters of the Trent & Mersey Canal Company. At the Crown Hotel in1776 Josiah Wedgwood held the company's first meeting and James Brindley was appointed surveyor-general[85]. The canal reached Stone in 1771 and during the 'lively celebrations' to mark the event the firing of canons caused one of the locks and a bridge to collapse[86].

Barely seven miles south of Stone, the canal reaches the attractive village of Weston-upon-Trent (not to be confused with the similar-sized village of the same name in Derbyshire). And it is here, some time between 1828 and 1830, that the Staffordshire part of the Sproston history began. Weston and its immediate environs became home to Thomas and Ann's family. Thomas would spend the rest of his life there, while still working the canals; and many of his children, too, would not stray far – including William. William spent most of his childhood and a good part of his adult life in or very close to Weston. It is where he met his future first wife, possibly at the Nag's Head, close to the canal, where she worked. The Nag's Head is no longer, although its old stables remain[87].

A guidebook of the time describes the village, together with its close junior neighbour, Shirleywich, as:

'… large and well built …, pleasantly seated on the north-east bank of the Trent … four and a half miles NE of Stafford… It has a commodious wharf on the Trent and Mersey Canal; and its parish, which has long been celebrated for its salt-works, contains 587 inhabitants, and 719 [acres] of fertile land, most of which belongs to Earl Ferrers, the lord of the manor… [The parish includes] Shirleywich, a small village, 1 mile SE of Weston, …so called from the family name of Earl Ferrers, and from its extensive salt-works, which were established upwards of two centuries ago'[88].

Middlewich, Shirleywich and Colwich share a word-ending with the towns of Droitwich, Nantwich and Northwich in Cheshire. The suffix *wich* or *wych* indicates the presence of salt in the local spring water, or more specifically the existence of salt workings[89]. And salt has its own contribution to the Sproston story.

The long-established salt-works at Middlewich are not the only sites in Cheshire where deposits of rock salt, dating from the Triassic period (over 200 million years ago), are to be found. The 'middle' in the name Middlewich refers to the town's location between Northwich and Nantwich at both of which the Romans extracted salt from the brine springs. From then on, salt was always in demand: in the days before refrigeration, salt was the principal means of preserving meat, fish and other foodstuffs. Extensive salt reserves around the Hassall Green/Betchton area led to the development of salt works at Rode Heath Rise (now replaced with a managed open space of meadows and woodland[90]). Rode Heath became a chief loading site on the Trent & Mersey for salt and the salt-derived products (soda, glass, soap) from the local industries which grew up in the district[91].

Some of the salt works in the area pre-dated the building of the canal (those at Church Lawton, for example, had started in the 17th century[92]), others followed as the canal afforded easier carriage to wider markets. It was the opening of the canal which led to the great expansion of the salt industry in the 18th and 19th centuries. The industrial process involved the formation of salt crystals through the evaporation of the brine pumped from below the ground. The crystals were then moulded into blocks which were dried in the large brick stove houses of the salt works. As well as distributing the product for the tables and cooking pots of Britain, the canal system became the first stage in the journey to global markets – Africa, India and Canada in particular[93]. With the Trent & Mersey providing access to expanding markets, it also made sense to develop the local production of ancillary products, so the economy of the area boomed. But salt was also important to the national economy and was a major contributor to government revenues. At one stage, the tax payable on the product reached over 90% of its selling price[94]. Today's business leaders who object so loudly to paying a tiny fraction of that in taxes really don't know they're born!

Farther south, in Staffordshire, the existing salt works at Shirleywich, though not on the same scale as some of the Cheshire works, were nonetheless similarly boosted by the arrival of the canal. As Shirleywich was close to the route of the canal, it required the digging of only a short branch cut for loading in order to take full advantage of the new means of transport. The expanded production provided an alternative to farm work for the local population. It would not have been an attractive proposition to everyone, however, as it could involve elongated periods of strenuous labour in dangerous conditions and extremes of temperature. In acknowledgement of their hard work, and presumably in addition to their wages, each employee, whatever their age, was entitled to a pint of beer at the end of each shift[95]. (Only one? It might have been from Joule's Brewery in Stone, though.)

Salt production at Shirleywich had first been established in the 17th century and peaked two hundred years later. An additional salt works in the village of Weston itself opened on the canal in the early 1820s following the discovery of a brine spring at the nearby village of Ingestre[96]. When brine pits were found a few miles away in Stafford, larger salt works were built there in the 1890s leading to the eventual closure of those at Shirleywich and Weston. Except for the loading arm of the canal, nothing remains of the Shirleywich works and the site is now a light industrial estate[97].

Thomas died in 1848 on the canal at Shirleywich. His wife, Ann, lived for a further 21 years. It seems that she may have continued to live and work on the canals for the place of her death is recorded as Autherly Junction, on the outskirts of Wolverhampton , where the Staffs & Worcestershire Canal meets the Shropshire Union Canal. Two years later, James – one of her sons and an older brother of William – died there, too[98].

By the mid-1850s, William is himself still working as a boatman. With his own family, he was based a stone's throw along the canal from Shirleywich at the bucolic-sounding Pasturefields, close to where the murdered Christina Collins was last seen. Today it is home to little more than a loose collection of light industries and a smattering of houses amidst rather flat countryside. There is however a protected Special Area of Conservation: Pasturefields Salt Marsh. This is described as *'the only known remaining example in the UK of a natural salt spring with inland salt marsh vegetation'*[99], a reminder of the source of the neighbourhood's former industrial glory.

During the industrial revolution, then, salt had become one of the principal cargoes of the multitude of narrowboats that travelled the Trent & Mersey, including those built or operated by Job Sproston and then his son, Thomas, and later by grandson William. So, if the route of the Trent & Mersey is the key to the Sproston move southwards, it is salt which helps to explain the places along the canal where successive generations of Sprostons chose to make their home.

And for William, at some time in 1862 or 1863, there was to be one more short canal journey to his final home in Little Haywood. On the way is Great Haywood where the Trent & Mersey is joined by the Staffordshire & Worcestershire Canal which crosses the River Trent by one of Brindley's aqueducts. It is here that a section of the river had previously been diverted to drive a corn mill. The existence of a mill at Great Haywood is recorded in Domesday Book[100] and there is evidence of a series of mills, on or near the same site, over the intervening centuries[101]. The arrival of the canals opened up further business opportunities and a paper mill was added to the original concern, a demonstration of how the canal era allowed new industries to develop from the old[102].

The canals were also responsible for rejuvenating and expanding what had been purely local industries. Just a mile away from Great Haywood, the Staffs & Worcester canal passes the village of Tixall. The local sandstone had been quarried since the 16th century and had been used in the building of Tixall Hall (where Mary Queen of Scots was imprisoned for a brief period in 1586). The stone had good water-resistant properties but its bulk and weight had restricted its use to buildings in the immediate vicinity. The coming of the canals provided a double boost to the industry: not only was the Tixall stone used in the construction of some of the canal architecture, the distance limitations were removed and the stone was soon being transported for use in building works much further afield[103].

Eventually William would own or rent wharves at Little Haywood and Sandon (a village on the Trent & Mersey a few miles to the north). These wharves were used to load and unload bulk goods – often coal – and were no doubt employed by William for his coal-delivery business but other local industries probably made use of them, too[104].

The national canal boom lasted until the 1830s when canals began to be superseded by the railways which would eventually meet many of industry's transport needs. But the canals did not become completely redundant until the era of lorry transport in the

*William Sproston's canal boats on the Trent & Mersey Canal at Little Haywood,
near the Navigation Inn, c.1890-1895. [Courtesy of Mrs L Davies]*

20th century and were still being used for transporting low-value
bulk goods until after the Second World War[105]. This is borne out
locally with reports of the Trent & Mersey through the Haywoods
still being busy in the early decades of that century:

> *'...water traffic was heavy and very competitive – boats would often
> move by night and horses were urged on relentlessly in order to get
> early to North Staffordshire and the Harecastle Tunnel.'*[106]

Narrowboats remained largely horse-drawn until after the First
World War and horses could still be seen on the towpaths of West
Midland canals in the 1960s[107]. Even though Staffordshire's canals
had continued to do well in the railway era of the 19th century (when
they were still used for transporting coal and iron), they were badly
affected – as were those in other regions – by the international
economic slump of the years between the two world wars[108]. Yet,
in the 1930s, an average of 32 boats a day were passing through
Haywood Lock, with varied cargoes, including coal, large glass

bottles of chemicals and pottery from Stoke-on-Trent (for the latter, heather from Cannock Chase was used for protective packaging)[109]. According to one historian, the final blow was the long winter of 1962-3 when the temperature stayed below zero almost constantly for months. Many of the remaining canal boats carrying freight became ice-bound while their road and rail competitors continued to operate[110].

Today, though, some canals have been given a new lease of life by the leisure industry. Pleasure craft began to appear in the 1950s but the industry did not immediately see the potential and many canals suffered from a lack of maintenance and repair[111]. Horse-drawn leisure craft may now be a rarity but many towpaths remain – to the delight of anglers and of walkers who prefer a flat terrain. In the summer, the shops, restaurants and pubs in the Great Haywood area benefit from the canal holiday trade, with about 600 boats a week passing through[112]. One of the leading pleasure boat hire companies also has a base in the village.

For the country as a whole, canals were crucial for the industrial revolution, providing its heavy transport and unlocking national and global markets. Regionally, they confirmed the West Midlands as an industrial heartland. For Staffordshire, The Trent & Mersey was a major contributor to its development and prosperity. Locally it helped define the shape and direction of the Haywoods and their neighbouring villages. For the Sprostons, from Job and his family down to William and his, the canal had been central to their lives – and in some cases their deaths. And the reach of the waterways did not stop with William. His two eldest sons to survive into adulthood, John and George, both followed their father in working as boatmen. John died at the age of 25 and the record searches for George have so far drawn a blank beyond the 1871 census. There is a family story, as yet uncorroborated, that on a bitterly cold winter's day the life of one of William's boatman sons was claimed by the icy waters of the canal.

If, following William's death, the canal was less important to the livelihoods of the Sproston family, it nonetheless had been the reason why Little Haywood became the family base. The canal-side Navigation Inn had been the birthplace of the later children, starting with Nel's father, Christopher, and home to all the surviving children at some stage. James was now the eldest son and, with his wife and children, he moved back into the family home. William's widow and most of his children and their families continued to live and make their living in the village. And it had all begun in the second half of the 18th century with Job's foresight in recognising the potential of the new Trent & Mersey (with a little help from the likes of Wedgwood, Brindley and thousands of navvies). But canals were not the only contributor to the revolution in communications and transport during the era of industrialisation. There were other crucial developments and changes that would also help to shape the nation's history and that of Little Haywood and its people.

Chapter 5

The Road to the Village... and Christopher and Ellen

In 2011, 1,901 people died in road traffic accidents in Great Britain[1]. This represents one fatality for every 17,885 registered vehicles[2]. This is not an especially comforting statistic – yet it reflects a considerable improvement in road safety over earlier decades. Eighty years before, there was one road death for every 2,800 vehicles. The number of people killed on the roads of Britain reached a peacetime peak of 8,000 in 1966, despite there being far fewer vehicles on the road than today[3]. And it was around this time that a section of new road opened which by-passed the villages of Colwich, Little Haywood and Great Haywood. It was a long time coming: in 1934 the parish council had written to the Ministry of Transport requesting such a solution following three fatal accidents[4].

Up until the construction of the by-pass, the villages straddled the busy main Chester to London road as it passed through this part of central Staffordshire where it shadows quite closely the line of the River Trent. The numbering of roads in Britain only began in the 1920s and a large stretch of the Chester-London road (today it runs from Chester to Kingsbury in Warwickshire) became the A51[5]. In Little Haywood the A51 went directly past Elizabeth's post office which stood exactly half-way between Stone, 12 miles to the north, and the cathedral city of Lichfield to the south. Occupying part of a three-storey house right at the centre of the village, it stood at the corner of Meadow Lane and the main London Road (on to which its front door opened). Its position in the village would have been a constant reminder of her husband's death as it was very close to the site of his road traffic accident. The building has since been demolished but there remain a few trees which once formed part of a substantial wood (mainly oak) behind the post office and along the main road[6].

During the first decade of the 20th century Elizabeth 2 retired and moved to a house nearby where she lived alone. Stepson Albert succeeded her as the village postmaster, although he continued to farm as well. He had married in 1902 and his wife took on the running of the grocery part of the business.

Across from the Post Office, forming the crossroads with Meadow Lane and the main road, is Coley Lane. At the turn of the century Christopher Sproston, the closest in age to younger brother Albert, was living a couple of hundred yards up this steep lane with his wife Ellen plus daughter Nel and her four brothers (eventually there would be seven children in the family). Also sharing the house were his wife's sister and her husband[7].

Christopher and Ellen had married on New Year's Eve 1887 at St Michael and All Angels Church in Colwich. Dating from the 13th century, the church stands on the main road and on the site of a much older Anglo-Saxon church[8]. It is where Christopher had been christened, where he would sing in the choir and become an enthusiastic campanologist. And it is where he and Ellen would both eventually be laid to rest, although no headstone marks the spot. Some of the grander and more famous of the parish are rather more ostentatiously remembered. They include members of the Anson family, of nearby Shugborough Hall, whose earthly remains occupy a vault inside the church itself. Thomas Anson, the first Earl of Lichfield, is commemorated in the east window. His brother, the famous circumnavigator of the globe Admiral George Anson, is buried there. Robert Wolseley of neighbouring Wolseley Hall, who fought on the side of the king in the Civil War, is also entombed in the church where there is an elaborate monument to his memory[9].

At the time of their marriage, Christopher was 24 and his wife, it is thought, a year older – although no record of the registration of her birth date has been found. Ellen was the first of five surviving children born to John and Mary Morris in or close to Castle Caereinion, near Welshpool in Wales. John worked as an agricultural labourer. There is a rumour that Mary spoke only Welsh although at some stage – probably in their late 30s – she and her husband moved to north-west Staffordshire and remained in the county until they died some 40 years later. Like her younger brothers and sisters, Ellen was brought up in a tiny community (consisting of only four houses) in rural mid-Wales, but before her marriage to Christopher she had worked as a general servant to a farmer in Shropshire[10].

Before the construction of Britain's motorway network (the first, short, section of which opened as the Preston bypass in the late 1950s), the main road through the villages had been an important thoroughfare since the Middle Ages, with *'many travellers, traders, seasonal workers and drovers with cattle pass[ing] through'*[11]. It had been part of the major road transport link between the capital and the north-west of England since the 14th century (in medieval times Chester was the port for Ireland[12]). It replaced the old Roman road which had linked Chester to London via Watling Street (which it joined in Shropshire, to the west of Staffordshire)[13].

The Romans are usually credited as the pioneers of road building, their first project being constructed in the 4th century BC and spanning more than 3,700 miles of western and southern Europe[14]. This seems a rather ambitious start: perhaps they practised on a couple of 'B' roads that we don't know about, first. Much earlier forms had been merely primitive trackways, used for trading goods, that date back to the stone age[15]. Roman roads were far more substantial – many lasted for centuries – and some of this country's original routes are still followed in sections of the modern road network, including Watling Street (the A5).

But in the centuries after the Romans departed, many of their roads fell into disrepair. There was no system of public administration to provide regular maintenance. Local parishes were given some responsibilities in 1555[16], but this still did not produce the sort of coordinated approach to maintaining the highways that was needed. One attempted solution was the turnpike trust. A group of business people (a trust) would petition Parliament to take over a stretch of roadway and offer to maintain or improve it or even to build a new one. In return road users would be stopped at a gate or barrier (pike) which could be turned to one side to give access to the road once payment had been handed over[17].

Although the concept of erecting spiked barriers on roadways to elicit tolls had begun in the 17th century, it was not until the 1700s that the turnpike trusts became well established and started to proliferate, particularly in the second half of that century[18].

Eventually, milestones (many of which can still be seen at roadsides) became compulsory on all turnpike roads as did the practice of erecting distance signs to nearest towns[19]. By 1830, more than a thousand trusts existed in England and there were 20,000 miles of turnpike roads[20]. In Britain as a whole, 3,300 stage coaches were in operation and speed of travel between some major cities increased markedly. In the early 1700s it had taken the best part of two weeks to get from London to Edinburgh by stagecoach. A century later this had been reduced to under two days[21]. The rate of reduction has been less impressive in the 200 years since then. Today, a national express coach trip from London Victoria to Edinburgh can take upwards of 18 hours[22], although the chance of unscheduled stops while Dick Turpin wannabes relieve passengers of their cash and personal possessions has reduced somewhat.

The better, more enlightened and more financially secure turnpike trusts did have a noticeable effect in improving the quality of roads and road-building generally. Some of the influential civil engineers of the time were employed as officials or consultants. John McAdam, for example, had been a trustee of an early Scottish turnpike company. In 1816, he was appointed as surveyor to the Bristol Turnpike Trust where he developed a particular system of road construction to which, famously, he lent his name – macadamisation. This system involved laying a top layer of broken stone directly on a raised bed of earth[23]. It was a method that turned out to be cheaper, if less strong, than that employed by his contemporary and fellow Scot, Thomas Telford, and was therefore particularly appealing to the cost-conscious trustees of the turnpike companies. Telford is perhaps even better known for his canal construction and for the design of bridges, such as the magnificent Menai Suspension Bridge linking Anglesey to the Welsh mainland. But he was also influential in refining the theories of the French pioneer road builder Tresaguet who had constructed roads in Paris in the 1750s and 1760s. One of Telford's chief contributions to road building was his emphasis on the importance of drainage. To this end, his road design had a top six-inch layer of compacted broken stone, sloping to each side from the centre, over a foundation of heavy rock[24]. Overcoming drainage problems had also been one of the achievements of the earlier road engineer Jack Metcalfe who, in the second half of the 18th century, had been responsible for building turnpike roads in some of the northern counties of England.

Focusing on the contributions of three or four well-known road-builders, however, invites the trap of the 'great man' theory of history. This is the idea that historical events and developments in each age are best explained through the actions of a few key individuals (usually men). It overlooks the roles played by the millions of ordinary men and women without whose labour the ideas and theories of the 'great men' would never be implemented. Metcalfe, Telford and McAdam were not actually road *builders* in the hands-on sense of the word (which would have been particularly difficult for Metcalfe in any case as he had been blind since the age of six). The roads of the 17th and 18th century were built, as they are today, by large teams of skilled, semi-skilled and unskilled workers.

'Great men', like all men and all women, are more instructively viewed as the products of their society and times. It is no surprise that Metcalfe, Telford and McAdam were all around at roughly the same time. The demand for civil engineers existed not because turnpike trustees suddenly developed a passionate intellectual interest in road surfaces and their substructures. Nor was it that members of the boards of turnpike trusts were public-spirited individuals keen to improve people's lives by providing the basis for a speedier and more comfortable means of transport. Rather, they wanted to make and to increase their profits.

And the turnpikes became one of the key areas for investment and re-investment during the earlier stages of the industrial revolution. Profits on a hitherto undreamt of scale became possible. So, although roads had been around a long time before industrialisation, many were now being transformed by the turnpikes and by the new engineering methods applied to road design and construction. By the last quarter of the 18th century, they were forming an important part of the new communications system which both fed and fed on the explosion of industry which was taking place in various parts of the country. Indeed, industrialisation relied on investment and innovation in transport keeping pace with the parallel developments in the production of goods[25].

The significant advances in the construction of Britain's road system in turn required considerable organisation for the upkeep of the highways. The expansion in both the number of new roads and the increased volume of traffic using them had to be sustainable. Large gangs of road repairers were needed for the continual renewal of worn surfaces. Delays in carrying out maintenance were not always avoided, as William Sproston was to discover on that fateful day in Little Haywood in March 1896. The jury at the inquest held at the Navigation Inn implied that an indirect cause of his death was the pile of stones covering half of the roadway which William had swerved to avoid. The broken granite stones were intended for nearby road repairs and the jury's verdict contained a rider that three weeks was too long for them to have lain there without being covered or unrolled[26].

Turnpike trusts were not universally popular. The introduction of direct charges for highway use is unlikely to have been welcomed by anyone previously using the road for free. But in some cases the sudden charging of tolls could have a marked effect on the living standards of particular groups and lead to pronounced discontent. In parts of west Wales such disquiet was expressed in the Rebecca Riots of 1839-1843. Tenant farmers in the area needed to make frequent use of the roads to take their products to market and to transport the lime commonly used as a soil improver[27]. Dressed as women, and calling themselves 'Rebecca and her daughters' (after a passage in Genesis, the first book of the bible), groups of men attacked and destroyed tollgates and tollhouses in protest against the imposition of the road charges.

The authorities dealt harshly with the protesters. Troops were called in to quell the rioters some of whom were sentenced to transportation to Australia for long periods, including life. Nonetheless, turnpike trusts in South-West Wales were abolished shortly after the riots[28], and the system of county roads boards which replaced them not only introduced fairer charges but also led to improved roads for the area.

In this sense, then, the rioters had been successful but, as with other protest movements of the first half of the 19th century (including the Swing Riots in southern England and Chartism), the Rebecca Riots were not just about a single issue (in this case, the turnpike tolls). They can also be seen as an expression of a more general discontent at the conditions of the time and at some of the other changes that were taking place. Unemployment, and the poverty it produced, had been growing. Radical changes to the Poor Law in 1834 had brought an imminent fear of the workhouse to working class families. (A month after the Carmarthen tollgates were attacked there was an attempt to burn down its workhouse, too[29].) The religious leanings of the vast majority of the small tenant farmers in the area were Nonconformist (protestant denominations which dissent from the established church) yet they were obliged to pay tithes to the Church of England. Resentment increased when payment in cash, rather than the previous payment in farm produce, was demanded[30].

But underlying all these changes were the ongoing social class divisions between the English-speaking Anglican landowners and the Welsh-speaking nonconformist small tenant farmers. Positions of authority – local magistrates, poor law officials, turnpike trustees – tended to be occupied by the former and these were the positions that were increasingly, and adversely, affecting the lives of those who worked the land[31].

Despite the work of the Trusts in improving and extending the road system, in some senses the roads played second fiddle to the canals[32]. Canals were far superior in transporting heavy and bulky materials (although even these had to be transported by road to get to and from the canal network). And, as well as endemic corruption[33], a major disadvantage of the system of turnpike trusts was its ad hoc and piecemeal method of maintaining or extending the road system. There was to be no overall supervision of the roads and turnpikes until the 19th century. It meant that the quality of each stretch of road depended on the engineering and financial competence of each separate group of individuals, or trust. This sort of problem, in many different contexts – be it hospitals, care homes or contracted-out refuse disposal services – is familiar enough to us in today's society with the prevailing orthodoxy of economic neo-liberalism (the belief that it is best to leave everything to the market whose self-correcting mechanism will somehow ensure that all is for the best in the best of all possible worlds). As a result, standards can and did vary enormously. And, of course, there would still be roads or sections of roads not turnpiked at all. In fact most roads, especially the vast majority of local roads, remained the responsibility of the parishes. By the late 19th century, the need for greater consistency, the formation of county, borough and district councils and the advent of motorised road traffic (even though the type of vehicle that killed off the pedestrian victim in Chapter 1 was still a rarity) finally saw off the turnpike trusts. Many trusts ended as a result of legislation passed in the 1870s[34]. The last one went out of business in 1895[35]. But half a century before then, the rapid development of a railway network had ensured that the coffin nail was becoming sharper than any pike as far as the future of the trusts was concerned.

After indicating some of the drawbacks and benefits of the turnpikes, the history writer and humourist John O'Farrell summarises their overall contribution:

> '...thousands of miles of road were built within a very short time... Suddenly Britain had some sort of transport infrastructure, people and goods could be easily moved around the country and trade and communications were vastly improved. Stagecoach companies established regular routes and timetables: "8 a.m., leave London for Bath; 12 noon, change horses at Maidenhead; 2 p.m. get held up at pistol point by lone highwayman..."'[36]

For passengers travelling between London and Chester, regular stagecoach services had become established by the mid-17th century, running weekly in the winter months and three times a week in summer[37]. Depending on the time of year, the journey took between four and six days so passengers needed to be refreshed, fed and bedded along the route. Coaching inns at various stages on the road therefore developed as regular stopping-off places.

In some respects, coaching inns were the more glamorous forerunners of the *Travelodge* but they also helped to form a strong image of what we have come to expect from a certain type of public house today. Pete Brown, the writer and historian of all things beery, argues that the British pub has its origins in three distinct types of establishment – each set up for a rather different purpose[38]. The *tavern* initially served wine and is of Roman origin. Situated at the side of the roads built by the Romans to facilitate troop movements, the *tabernae* provided resting places – and wine – for the passing soldiers. In London and a few other more prosperous places, the tavern survived the departure of the Romans and much later began to sell beer as well as wine[39]. The *alehouse* stems from a time when many people baked their own bread and, using the same yeast, brewed their own beer. Sometimes this would be done communally. A stick – an ale stake – would be displayed outside the house to inform the neighbours when the beer was ready to drink. Some places would gain a reputation for good brews and start to charge locals for the privilege of drinking their beer – eventually becoming alehouses[40]. The *inn* has provided accommodation, stabling and food – as well as beer – for travellers since the sort of pilgrimage depicted in Chaucer's *Canterbury Tales* first became popular. The arrival of the turnpikes and public stagecoach gave rise more specifically to the coaching inns that sprung up along the main long-distance passenger routes[41].

As it was one of the country's major thoroughfares, it is not surprising, then, that the London-Chester road attracted many coaching inns and, indeed, some of the first turnpike trusts. The Staffordshire section of the road was turnpiked in 1729[42] and the county of Staffordshire became one of the most turnpiked, by mileage, in England[43]. By the 1770s, road improvements between the two cities had cut the travelling time to two days[44]. The coaching inns along the route would vary in size. Some of the smaller establishments served only as places for a change of horses, a requirement that became more frequent as the speed of coach travel increased. The more lucrative business of the larger inns, on the other hand, would meet all requirements for travellers' overnight stays[45]. The Staffordshire town of Stone was a major staging post and, at one time, 38 stage coaches were passing through each day[46]. The still existing Crown (where Josiah Wedgwood held the inaugural meeting of the Trent & Mersey Canal Company) is a good example of a larger coaching inn there.

A trustee of one of the earlier turnpike companies in his native

Wales was the naturalist and travel writer Thomas Pennant[47]. In 1780, he wrote in varying detail about the towns and villages on his road journey between Chester and London[48]. The first half of his journey follows closely what is now the A51, with short detours to stately homes and other places of antiquity in which Pennant was particularly interested[49]. When not a guest of one his aristocratic friends or acquaintances, he may have made use of the coaching inns on his travels. He would have regarded them as a poor substitute, however. They could be quite dangerous places and his chances of being robbed, or worse, would be considerably higher[50].

After crossing the border between Cheshire and Staffordshire, he passed through *'the little town of Stone'*[51] and continued to the village of Sandon, describing in some genealogical detail its manorial history. From there he diverts northwards from 'the great road'[52] for a couple of miles in order to visit Chartley Manor. It was here that Mary, Queen of Scots, had spent some of the later months of her imprisonment before being moved to Fotheringay where her head and body finally parted company in 1587. Pennant provides one of the last descriptions of the decaying former grandeur of the Manor house as a year after his visit much of it was burnt to the ground[53]. A smaller replacement was built but this, too, was destroyed by fire in the 19th century[54]. Whether there were any suspicions, on either occasion, about spurious insurance claims is not recorded, but the third rebuilding effort has so far remained intact. After a quick look at the remains of nearby Chartley Castle and the parish church at Stowe, Pennant:

'... *hastened [back] to the* Chester *road, which I reached at the hamlet of* Wych [Shirleywich], *in the parish of* Weston *on the Trent, whose spire steeple appears at a small distance on the other side of the road.'*[55]

The church espied from a distance by Pennant is the Parish Church of St Andrews where, 68 years later, boatman Thomas Sproston – father of William, grandfather of Christopher and great-grandfather of Nel – would be buried, joining a son and a grandson who had died before him[56]. Its 13th century tower is thought to be one of the finest in the county and major restoration works in the second half of the 19th century revealed the church's Norman origins[57].

Most of the ancient parish of Weston was part of the extensive Chartley Estate until it was sold by Earl Ferrers in 1904[58]. Once a forest clearing on the edge of the estate, the village itself, with its large green, fits snugly into the south-west quadrant formed by the crossroads of the old London-Chester and Shrewsbury-Derby roads. Over the past half-century, it has featured frequently among the prize winners of Staffordshire's Best Kept Village competitions. Unlike some of the county's villages, it has not grown greatly in size since Christopher's mother and father met there in the 1840s. New houses have been built but the A51 to the east and the canal (in particular) and river running in parallel to the west seem to have acted as boundary limits to the sprawling developments seen elsewhere.

Far more interested in aristocratic history than in the evidence of the emerging industrial society unveiling before him, Pennant nevertheless does refer briefly to the salt works of Shirleywich before journeying a further two miles along the London Road to reach Great Haywood. He has little to say specifically about the village itself other than noting that it was

> '*bestowed by Roger de Meland, alias Long Epee, a worthless prelate, in the reign of Henry III on his valet Roger de Aston; whose family made it their residence, till the marriage of a descendant with the heiress of Tixal, occasioned it to remove to the new acquisition*'[59]

There is no mention of any of the three coaching inns in the vicinity. Despite its proximity to the coaching inns of Stone, the Lamb and Flag at Little Haywood, though smaller, also catered for overnighters[60]. The Clifford Arms at Great Haywood and the Wolseley Arms at Wolseley Bridge were at one time important coaching inns, too. The accommodation sides of their businesses probably suffered, however, as travel times lessened. At the time of Pennant's journey it seems that one of these local establishments (which one, unfortunately, is not reported), had developed a somewhat fearsome reputation:

'Travellers who put up there on their way to Lichfield or Stafford disappeared, leaving no trace; suspicion was aroused, but nothing could be proved against the evil couple of the inn. One man who disappeared was a merchant in silk. Many years afterwards, when new stalls were being put in the stables, two skeletons were found under the flooring.'[61]

The Navigation Inn, however, was more reminiscent of an alehouse and it did not survive long into the 20th century. The very last pint was served on 28 December 1912. This was the date that the pub (licensee – James Sproston; owner – the Earl of Lichfield) closed and was 'referred for compensation' under the 1904 Licensing Act[62]. Just like its counterpart a century or so later, the government at the end of the 19th century had become increasingly concerned about the extent of alcohol consumption in the country. More precisely, then as now, it was bothered about excessive drinking among the working classes. It decided that the problem lay in the number of premises licensed to sell beer. So the Licensing Act, designed to reduce the number of pubs, was introduced. Licensees whose premises closed could apply for financial compensation[63]. Unlike the Lamb & Flag and the Red Lion, the Navigation Inn, tucked away down Meadow Lane, did not have the advantage of the through traffic on the London-Chester road. The future for other sources of custom would not have looked promising. The number of thirsty agricultural workers was likely to continue to decrease rather than the reverse. And, although the Haywood stretch of the Trent & Mersey was surviving better than many on the nation's canal network, perhaps James could see a downward trend in demand for beer from the boats, too. Whatever the reasons, he was calling it a day as far as the public house side of the business was concerned.

The ending of James's licence, together with many others up and down the country, came at a time when the temperance movement, which had been growing throughout the Victorian era, was nearing the peak of its political clout[64]. It was particularly influential among sections of the Liberal Party, the party in office from 1906 to 1914. The difference the Navigation Inn's closure made to drinking levels in the village or on the canal boats is not recorded, however. There would still be plenty of alternative drinking places in the vicinity.

Attempts by the authorities to control alcohol consumption go back over a thousand years but rarely have they produced the desired effect[65]. The 21st century remedy for the evils of mass drinking differs from that prescribed in 1904. Following the example of the Scottish Parliament, the UK Tory-led coalition government announced in 2013 that it intended to introduce a minimum price per unit of alcohol. The powerful drinks lobby – including the good friends of the Conservative Party, the brewers – were not too keen on the idea and it has yet to be introduced. As Pete Brown has demonstrated, over the centuries the official attitude to alcohol has always been ambivalent. The government fears the masses getting out of (its) control but it also wants to protect a valuable source of tax income[66].

In 1922 Elizabeth 2 died, aged 83, leaving £1,081 in her will[67]. In her relatively long life she had seen a lot of changes – locally, nationally and globally. And some of the greatest changes had occurred over her final decade. The direct and indirect military and civilian casualties of the Great War ran into the tens of millions. The health of millions of those who were not killed was permanently ruined and the effects on families and communities are incalculable. In Britain, it has often been said that most families would have experienced at least one war-time casualty – and the Sproston family was no exception. The numbers who died from the 1918 flu pandemic (known as 'Spanish flu') were even higher, although a substantial proportion of military deaths was also due to the disease.

Major economic and political changes followed the end of the First World War, some of which would mark out the key features of British society, and shape the lives of its people, for the next couple of decades. The years between the two world wars proved prosperous for some, dismal and even devastating for many more. More positively, four years before her death, Elizabeth would be among the first generation of women able to vote at a British general election. Although full voting equality on gender lines would not be forthcoming for a further ten years, many thought that the Representation of the People Act of 1918 was a recognition of the changing position of women in society and that it represented an important breakthrough for women's political and social rights after a long struggle. Others were more sceptical about its wider emancipatory impact.

During the 19th century, the franchise (the right to vote) had gradually been extended from a privileged minority of less than 5% of the adult population to the majority of adult males. Provided they were categorised as 'householders', men of all social classes were now able to exercise what is often seen as a basic democratic right – as long as they were, well, male. In parliamentary elections, however, all women – whatever their class position – were still denied the vote.

A small number of women, and a few men, had long supported the idea of votes for women but it was not until the later part of 19th century, that the campaign began to gather momentum. In the early stages, it was largely confined to middle class women who had seen the vote being given to a class of men they viewed as *'less educated ... [and] of lower social status ... whilst they remained disenfranchised'*[68]. But, in the period leading up to the First World War, the demand for women's suffrage (another word for the right to vote) developed into *'a major confrontation with the ... state'*[69].

In 1897, local groups from different parts of the country joined together to form the National Union of Women's Suffrage Societies. The NUWSS used law-abiding methods of campaigning to press for an extension of the franchise to women. Their efforts went into lobbying (attempting to persuade) MPs, organising petitions and holding rallies. Six years later, Emmeline Pankhurst and her daughters Christabel and Sylvia formed a rival organisation – the Women's Social and Political Union (WSPU) – in the belief that the tactics of the NUWSS were insufficiently robust to achieve the desired outcome. The WSPU favoured the use of public protests and direct action which they carried out with increasing frequency and intensity in the years leading up to the First World War.

Today's historians often distinguish between the two groups by referring to members of the NUWSS as suffragists and those in the WSPU as suffragettes but, at the time, the former was an umbrella label for any supporter of votes for women. As planned, the actions of the suffragettes attracted the greater publicity. Arrests

73

and imprisonments escalated. In 1909, the WSPU introduced a policy whereby suffragettes in prison would go on hunger strike. The brutal response of the prison authorities was to force-feed the strikers. When this seemed to be producing public sympathy for the suffragettes, the government introduced legislation which became known as the 'Cat and Mouse Act'. This enabled the release of hunger strikers from prison when they reached the verge of starvation and their re-incarceration once their health began to recover.

Various attempts to legislate for women's suffrage had failed to get through Parliament and the WSPU stepped up its campaign. The earlier activities of heckling speakers at public meetings and smashing windows continued but were supplemented by acts of arson, bombings and physical attacks on government ministers[70]. Over time the suffragette movement had changed from being a pressure group of persuasion to *'an underground organisation...[with] an elite corps trained in urban sabotage'*[71]. When war broke out in 1914, however, the leaders publicly abandoned the policy of direct action, pledging instead to help the war effort. During the war women took over much of the work previously done by men who had enlisted in the forces. In 1918 Parliament gave the vote to women over 30 (men could vote once they had reached the age of 21). The first general election at which women were able to exercise this right was held within weeks of the signing of the armistice (the official end of the war).

It might be tempting, therefore, to see female enfranchisement as the reward granted by a grateful government for women's war-time work in the nation's factories. But there are reasons to doubt this view. Women were not new to the work place. Working class women had formed an important part of the labour force since the beginnings of the industrial revolution, and even before. For a long time they had worked in agriculture, in domestic service and in textile production. Demand for women's labour in the factories increased in the 19th century as successive pieces of legislation excluded the employment of children in more and more industries. Though a very slow process, some professions, such as pharmacy and journalism, were gradually opening their doors to middle class women by the final quarter of the century. Furthermore, it was women under the age of 30 who formed a large proportion of those employed during the war, and yet this age group was specifically excluded from the 1918 legislation. Although favourable press coverage of women's war work would no doubt have helped the cause, some historians believe that women would not have gained the vote when they did without the militant tactics of the suffragettes. There is an acknowledgement, however, that the more violent elements of the later stages (1912-1914) probably harmed rather than furthered the campaign and may have done little to alter the government position at the time[72].

When the first women's suffrage societies had begun in the 1860s, it is probably true to say that most of their members saw the vote as an end itself. At the time of the WSPU's formation, however, Emmeline Pankhurst had implied that achieving the vote for women was the means (political enfranchisement) to a broader end (the social emancipation of women). Daughter Sylvia (who was later to leave the WSPU for another organisation more in tune with her feminist-socialist politics) had always *'seen the franchise in the perspective of wider social changes'*[73]. Although by 1918 some inroads had been made into the patriarchal nature of British society, women still occupied a subordinate position to that of men across most areas of social life: economic, intellectual, moral and, of course, political. Average rates of pay for women were less than half that for men. Educational opportunities were greater for males, particularly in higher education. The marked differences in expectations of and constraints on the behaviour of men and of women, characteristic of the Victorian era, were only beginning to loosen. And, although the inequalities in one area of political life had now been reduced, they had not been eradicated completely and opportunities for women to participate in national politics had only just started.

In 1928, a decade after the general election at which women had first voted, legislation was introduced giving all women equal voting rights to men. Virtually all adults 21 and over were now entitled to vote for their Members of Parliament. The original wider intentions of the WSPU seem to have been lost along the way and the organisation had disbanded in 1918. As Martin Pugh has pointed out, it was left to a much later generation, with the women's movement of the 1960s and 1970s, to pick up the campaign for wider feminist objectives[74]. Enfranchisement for women had been achieved, but not their emancipation.

Women were not unknown in business, as the life of Elizabeth 2 shows, and within the working class single women were often in paid work. If and once married, however, the common assumption was that their priority should be to raise children and look after the home. This assumption prevailed even if the woman continued in paid employment after marriage. It was also to last long after women had gained the vote. After her years in domestic service to the family of a farmer, the life experienced by Ellen Morris following her marriage to Christopher Sproston would not have been so different. Immediately taking on the role of farmworker's wife, it was to be over three years until the birth of the first child. The baby was named Christopher. In apparent blissful ignorance of the domestic confusion it can cause, it is still fairly commonplace to name the first born after a parent, particularly if it is a boy. It is also not unusual for the child subsequently to be referred to by another name – as a way of circumventing the confusion created in the first place. This was the case with Christopher, who became known by his middle name Hazel – which is not so usual.

Hazel was followed – in regular intervals of two to three years – by six more children (including twins) until 1904 when the family was complete. In the early years of the 20th century, probably in or about 1903, the family moved house. They moved down the hill and around the corner, from the rented farmhouse in Coley Lane to an end-terrace cottage on Main Road. This was on the main London – Chester road. So, the A51, as it became known, continued to impinge on the lives of the Sproston family and was central – in more ways than one – to the village of Little Haywood. For centuries, the road that cuts through the village had conveyed passing traffic, of increasing sophistication, and had helped determine the shape of village development long before the canal which runs parallel to it.

Although canals had the edge over roads in the transport of heavy and bulky goods, the improvements to the country's major roads which followed the coming of the turnpikes were certainly important to Britain's, and to Staffordshire's, industrialisation and were usually better for passenger traffic. But the heyday of the roads, when their economic potential would be freed from the limitations of 'horse and wagon'[75], was yet to come. In the meantime, another great breakthrough in transport was to shake the nation – and to leave further permanent marks on the village, too.

Chapter 6

To the Village by Rail... and the Magnificent Seven

'*Residents say HS2 will "devastate" community*'. So ran a local press headline in January, 2012[1]. The accompanying article referred to residents from Little Haywood and Colwich alarmed that the second phase route of the proposed high-speed rail link was likely to pass through their villages. Detailed plans published a year later, however, revealed a government-preferred route a little to the north[2]. But even this route is considered too close for comfort, necessitating the construction of a viaduct over the narrowboat marina at Great Haywood[3].

The residents' fears had been understandable. It would not have been the first time that railway lines have sliced through the parish – nor even the second. In 1847 the Trent Valley Railway between Rugby and Stafford was opened as part of the major London and North Western trunk line[4]. Then, within the same year, the villages were dealt the second part of a double whammy when work began on the North Staffordshire Railway (or *Knotty*, as it became known, after the county emblem, the Stafford Knot)[5]. Opening in 1849, this line was built to run from Macclesfield in Cheshire through the Potteries to Colwich. And it is at Colwich where, from the west, the two lines converge and where a station was built in 1847[6].

The clearest image of the impact that the successive communications revolutions of the past two to three centuries have had on Little Haywood can be gained by taking a short walk along Meadow Lane. Approaching from the south, or Cannock Chase end, you turn into the lane from the A513, the Stafford-Rugeley road, and cross the River Trent by means of Weetman's Bridge before going under the West-Coast main line (the old Trent Valley line). A little farther on you pass over the hump-back canal bridge and then almost immediately under the low-slung railway bridge where above you trains still run on the old North Staffordshire line. The road here not only significantly narrows and loses its footpath but also takes a severe dip. This allows you to continue safely on your way without fear of head-bridge contact, providing of course you are not run down by passing motorists fearful that the roofs of their vehicles may not make it through in a similarly unscathed fashion. After once again opening out a little and regaining its footpath, the lane reaches the main road (the old A51) which, in a much earlier age, did its own share of village slicing.

For anyone who has not been counting, and if the roads at each end are included, Meadow Lane is crossed six times – by two roads, two railways, a river and a canal – yet is not much more than a mile long. This part of the parish is therefore effectively divided into five segments. In a narrow strip, and squeezed between the canal and the *Knotty* line, lies Navigation Farmhouse (previously the Inn) and its outbuildings. The other side of this second railway was agricultural land until houses were built in the second half of last century. And it was possibly this land that led to Christopher and Ellen's house move.

The six-roomed Ivy Cottage was smaller than the house in Coley Lane, yet the family was growing. So why the move? The most likely reason is a change in Christopher's employment status. At some stage after leaving the parental home at Navigation Inn, where he no doubt also assisted his father on the farm, Christopher became a tenant farmer on his own account in Coley Lane. The adjacent house may have come with the tenancy. In the early 1900s, and probably coinciding with the short move from Coley Lane to Main Road, he acquired a smallholding in Little Haywood and was able to continue to dairy farm. In trade directories up to 1940, by which time he was 77 years old, he continued to be listed as a 'cowkeeper'. The cows were kept for their milk which Christopher, in later life assisted by his fourth son, Albert, would deliver on foot. Milk from the larger farms would be delivered by pony-and-trap, but the man with a yoke on his shoulders, from which hung two pails, was to remain a familiar sight in the village for a long time[7].

But Christopher had another string to his bow. Continuing another family tradition, he delivered coal around the villages – and for this he did use a horse and cart. This was not a great idea as Christopher had a health condition: he could fall asleep in an instant. Without warning he could be face-down in his plate at meal times. Far less amusing to his family, the more so given the fate of his own father, he would sometimes drop off at the reins. It is perhaps why wife Ellen or son Albert would accompany him on his coal deliveries whenever possible[8].

Despite the narcoleptic tendencies and the small scale of his enterprises, however, Christopher managed to survive the economic depression of the 1930s during which milk prices crashed and some local farmers switched from cattle to sheep[9]. But collapses in milk prices were not new. They had hit a low in the years immediately following the First World War, and at least in part this had been due to a government smallholding initiative. Using land, of variable quality, acquired from large landowners, smallhold farms of 20-30 acres were made available through the county councils. Designed initially to help disabled ex-servicemen into farming, the scheme became applied more widely. There was no requirement for applicants to have previous agricultural experience or training and they were no doubt encouraged by the popular sentiment that *given a roll of barbed wire and a milking stool'* they too could become farmers[10]. Many of these new small enterprises subsequently failed, but one consequence of the initiative was a surplus in the milk supply with prices dropping as low as 1/2d (0.2p in decimal currency) a gallon[11].

In Little Haywood, and no doubt in many other dairy farming villages, some of the surplus would continue to go into local butter and cheese making. A local resident later recalled some details of such activity during and after the First World War:

'Butter was made locally on the farms and when paper ran out it was wrapped in large butter-dock leaves cut from the riverside. In the 1920s green cheese was made at one local farm, parsley made the colouring and when this ran out potato leaves were used. The cheese was sold at the back door to miners during the Miners' Strike'[12].

Christopher and Ellen persevered, however, and, as a granddaughter remembers, their smallholding allowed them to rear other animals, too:

'They kept pigs, cows and chickens, so we always had eggs and meat. Gran used to hang a pig in her cellar and cure it, then divide it up for the family and as gifts for neighbours.'[13]

The memory is specifically about village life during the Second World War (1939-1945). Up to the outbreak of the war, and probably also during it, milking in Little Haywood was typically still done by hand[14]. Given the size of his own set-up, it is highly likely that milking by hand continued on Christopher's smallholding until his death in 1948.

It was only a short stroll from Ellen and Christopher's new home to the smallholding – just enough time for the first smoke of the day on the way to work. The land he farmed was in Meadow Lane. It would have extended right up to the back of the Navigation Inn were it not for the railway line separating the smallholding from his birthplace and childhood home.

Both railways had become part of the village before Christopher's time and even before father William had moved to Meadow Lane. They had been built during or as a result of the hyperactivity of investment known as 'railway mania' that had gripped the nation in the mid-1840s. Over a very short period, the major arteries of a national railway network were functioning and at the height of the railway era there was barely a town in the country that did not have access to train services – and many villages had their own station, too.

Unlike the canals and the roads, whose histories can be said to have spread over millennia, the railways were a new phenomenon – at least in anything resembling the form that would be recognised today. With some justification, it may be claimed that the railway era proper did not begin until the opening of the Liverpool-Manchester line in 1830. This would identify the railway as a true child of the industrial revolution – and a rather late one at that. It is known that wooden rails or planks were used to assist the movement of trucks pushed by miners in the ironworks of the Black Forest from at least the early 16[15] century[15]. It has even been suggested that a similar idea was employed in Ancient Greece to move boats across narrow strips of land[16]. In Britain, the concept would eventually extend to the use of horses to pull coal carts from the mines to the nearest waterways for onward transmission by boat. From the second half of the 18th century, iron rails and wheels started to replace wood on these wagon-ways[17]. And, after James Watt had adapted Newcomen's steam pump (designed to prevent flooding in the mines) for a wider range of functions, the steam engine could be employed to pull coal carts by cable. But at this stage of technological development, the engines were still static – and fixed.

Soon after mining engineer Richard Trevithick had experimented with the first mobile steam engines, George Stephenson had sufficiently developed his locomotives to enable the opening of the first steam-hauled public railway in 1825[18]. The line ran from the coalfield at Darlington to Stockton on the River Tees as its original purpose was the transport of coal to coastal shipping outlets. By this time the use of steam power in Britain's mills and factories was widespread and the demands of industry for coal to produce this steam seemed almost insatiable. The existing forms of transport were too ponderous and slow to cope with the stage that industrialisation had reached. Business people were open to alternatives. They were on the lookout in particular for a way of moving bulky goods at low cost but more quickly and efficiently than the canals or roads could manage.

Even though the Stockton-Darlington railway had the benefit of Stephenson's locomotives, the line was still making use of horses and stationary steam engines as well. Nevertheless, its potential for a higher intensity of traffic and reduced costs[19] was sufficient to whet the appetite of a motley band of merchants, bankers, industrialists, slave traders and politicians from England's North-West. This group of local movers and shakers could see the tremendous potential of a railway link in accelerating the movement of goods, particularly those associated with the production of cotton goods, between the rapidly growing manufacturing centre of Manchester and the principal west-coast port of Liverpool. These two places were of continuing importance to Britain's industrial revolution.

As with the canals and turnpike trusts, an individual Act of Parliament was needed to allow each railway project to go ahead. There were setbacks and objections along the way. Lord Sefton of Croxteth Hall, for example, vigorously opposed plans to route the line across a corner of his country estate. Nonetheless, approval for the Liverpool & Manchester Railway was granted in 1826. The grand opening ceremony took place on 15 September 1830. In the meantime, George Stephenson and his team of engineers had overcome a series of major problems posed by the hills and the valleys and the acres of wetland that lay along and beneath the route of the line. Solutions included the construction of more than sixty bridges and viaducts and a floating raft to support a railway embankment over a swamp[20].

The opening day featured Stephenson's *Rocket* – designed by George's son, Robert. At 29 mph, it was twice as fast as the older locomotives which were also being used to pull trains of guests along the line. The whole event attracted a good deal of interest with the world's press in attendance and spectators lining the route (although the reported one-million strong crowd is probably hyperbolic). The day was marked and marred, however, by railway's first passenger fatality. Sir William Huskisson, a local MP and former Cabinet Minister, was attempting to talk to the Prime Minister, The Duke of Wellington, when he was scythed down by a passing steam engine. Ironically, Huskisson had been a major supporter of the railway and may have been attempting to enthuse his leader who was apparently less impressed by the new means of transport. The irony was complete when it was realised that the engine that had run Sir William over was the *Rocket*[21].

For some historians, the Liverpool & Manchester represented the start of the railway age because it combined for the first time all the defining features by which classic rail transport would long be recognised:

'...*the double track of iron rails for the regular public conveyance of passengers and freight by steam-locomotive haulage between major cities, with all the accessories of stations, signals, bridges, tunnels, cuttings, embankments and trains of first-, second- and third-class carriages.*'[22]

Even though constitutional pedants might complain that neither Manchester nor Liverpool had yet officially been granted city status, it is the inter-city ingredient that is commonly emphasised. The distance between the two conurbations is only 30 miles yet the Liverpool & Manchester Railway soon became the model for plans to link cities far further apart. Within a few years, parliamentary approval had been given for the first major trunk lines of what, a couple of decades later, would be a truly national network.

The first of these nationally important trunk lines went through Staffordshire. Opened in 1837, the Grand Junction Railway from Merseyside to Birmingham passed through Stafford and the Black Country[23]. In the following year, the line was extended to London in what has been described as the major civil engineering project of its time. As its chief engineer, Robert Stephenson had overall responsibility for the construction of the eight tunnels, 150 bridges, five viaducts and 17 stations along the 112-mile route of the Birmingham-London line[24]. Within a decade, many other trunk lines had been built including the Trent Valley Railway which, in bypassing Birmingham, provided a more direct route from London to the North of England[25].

As with the building of the canals, the proper heroes of the age of railway construction were the mobile gangs of navvies. Taking the period from the 1820s to the early 1900s as a whole, millions of men[26] were hired to dig out the cuttings, excavate the tunnels and level the land. The work was done by hand and with the most rudimentary equipment – plus a liberal and often enthusiastic use of gunpowder. Within the gangs, the navvies worked in pairs, one cutting into earth or rock with a pick, the other shovelling the dislodged material into their truck. An experienced pair would shift an average of 30 tons a day. The hours and intensity of labour demanded from the navvies by the contractors meant that it could take a year for new recruits to reach the levels expected of them[27].

For some, this daily backbreaking toil would continue throughout their entire working lives. For more than a few, though, working lives would be short: the building of the world's first railway network would be paid for in thousands of deaths[28]. High in the Pennines is the isolated graveyard of St James Chapel in the village of Woodhead. Beyond the graveyard walls is a bare field which contains 26 unmarked graves. On this desolate hillside lie the remains of just some of the navvies killed while digging out the three-mile railway tunnel beneath. As the presenter of a BBC2 television documentary commented, it is *'not much of a monument to the men who helped to build modern Britain'*[29]. In addition to the high death toll throughout the country, many more navvies would be permanently disabled by accidents at work. Yet, not until the end of the century was there any legal obligation on employers to compensate for death or injury[30].

Like those of the canal era, then, the railway navvies experienced some of the worst working conditions imaginable. Living conditions were similarly primitive, sometimes consisting of a series of turf-covered burrows in embankments of earth together forming small shanty towns[31]. In 1846, calls from the public health reformer, Edwin Chadwick, for improvements to the disgraceful state of the navvies' camps run by the railway companies fell on deaf parliamentary ears[32]. On the face of it, the navvies could appear to be relatively well rewarded financially. They could earn at least twice the pay of an agricultural labourer. But the greater amount of food required to sustain the unremittingly strenuous nature of their work, combined with the extortionate 'truck' or 'tommy' shop system and the rents paid for their squalid accommodation (both controlled by their employers), would seriously reduce the real value of the navvies' wages[33].

As with the canals before them, the construction of the railways in Britain was left to private enterprise. This was not normally the case elsewhere. Greater degrees of central planning were employed in the countries that followed in their railway development. This meant they were better placed to avoid some of the silly results of the unrestrained and over-zealous competition that a later government enquiry would refer to as a 'riot of individuality'[34]. Examples of British railway stupidity abound – whether it is the different gauges of line that would cause unnecessary transhipments or the six different railway companies all operating from the same Manchester stations and competing for the same passengers; the lack of standardisation of rolling-stock components or the parallel sets of line built by rival companies (as happened, for instance, between Birmingham and Wolverhampton[35]). Parliament was in no hurry to establish greater uniformity as so many of its members were directors of railway companies[36] and stood to benefit handsomely if the gambles of their businesses paid off.

Despite the excesses and duplications, however, the inventiveness, the engineering skills, and the labour that went into the construction of the first railways amounted to a remarkable achievement. During its period of industrialisation, mid-19th century Britain had been through a hundred years of remarkable achievements. In recognition of these developments, a massive, hugely ambitious celebration was staged in London's Hyde Park in 1851. Although ostensibly an international event with examples from all over the globe, the Great Exhibition was really a gigantic advertisement to the rest of the world of what the British people had been up to over the previous century. It was apt that examples of steam locomotives were on display as, without the railways, the exhibition could not have taken place. They had been responsible for transporting the vast majority of the six million visitors during the Exhibition's run. By the time it closed towards the end of the year, most of Britain's trunk routes were in place and a total of 7,000 miles of railway lines in operation[37]. Nearly all the nation's major towns and cities were now linked into the new transport network. Journey times could be counted in hours, rather than in days as they had been with the stage coach travel of just 20 years before[38].

It was a formidable transformation in such a short period of time. At the start, there had been the almost inevitable wave of dire warnings of the 'if God had meant us to travel at 29 mph He'd have given us turbo-charged undergarments' type. Some artists and writers depicted the railway as the work of the devil[39]. Prime Minister Wellington was not a fan, believing (correctly as it turned out) that it would only 'encourage the lower classes to travel about'[40].

The initial fears were soon dampened, however, as people with cash to spare began to spot the opportunities for some serious unearned income. Initially, railway profits were created not so much from the transport of raw materials and freight, as had been expected, as from carrying passengers. And it was this passenger traffic that killed off long-distance coaching, and did so quite abruptly[41]. The era of the coaching inn also came to a swift end – but was replaced by the railway hotels that were built in many major towns and cities[42]. It was not until the early 1850s that freight started to become more lucrative for the railway companies[43]. The older forms of transport – the roads and the canals – continued to be used alongside the railways for carrying goods. The railway companies responded by strategically buying up canal shares and by the mid-1860s more than a quarter of the country's inland waterway mileage was in railway company ownership[44]. But intermodal investment was not only one-way. Canal companies were aware of the competitive threat posed to their core business and showed that they were prepared to invest in the railway companies. The directors of the Trent & Mersey Canal company went one step further. They changed the company into a railway company, the North Staffordshire (the Knotty), but still kept open the canal for the carriage of bulk goods[45].

But it was the new form of people-travel that first captured the public's imagination. It was in this that the railway was proving popular, with passengers and investors alike. Although the writers and artists of the time were sometimes hostile or ambivalent to the products and processes of the industrial revolution, many were nonetheless keen to supply their own individual takes on the new phenomenon of the railway. One of the more striking and lasting impressions was provided by JMW Turner in his painting Rain, Steam and Speed, first exhibited in 1844. The focus of the image is the immense power of the locomotive pulling a train over Maidenhead railway bridge above the Thames, forcibly casting aside the effects of the weather and nature just as the railway and the power of industry confines to history all previous economic and social forms.

From the outset, the railway developers were to have one big advantage denied to other businesses at the time. They were not legally restricted in the number of permitted investors for each project. Additionally, there was the protection of limited liability: investors could not lose more than the amount they had put in[46]. Railway shares were thus an attractive proposition to the would-be investor and the railways did require capital – massive amounts of it. For the investing classes, railways were the new canals – and more. The 1830s were boom time with the result that by 1843, more than 2,000 miles of line were in operation. Fortunes were being made, even bigger fortunes promised and by the mid-1840s *'the country was gripped by a speculative fever'* of investment[47]. The fashion for gambling in shares spread like a disease through the upper and middle classes. Parliament was kept busy passing Railway Acts by the bucketful. In just three years, 9,000 miles of new line were approved[48]. This was 'railway mania'. A somewhat baffled William Wordsworth complained that the nation had become *'an asylum of railway lunatics'*[49].

Substantial amounts of the money invested in the railways came from slavery – or, more precisely, from its abolition. When the practice was outlawed in its colonies in 1833, the British government paid out staggering amounts of compensation to the slave owners (not to the slaves). A total equivalent to 40% of the Treasury's annual budget was doled out to these recipients, many of them absentee owners living in Britain and many of them already exceedingly wealthy[50]. For example, John Gladstone, the father of William who later became Prime Minister, was given almost £107,000 for the 2,508 slaves he had owned. According to one estimate, this represents £83 million in 2013 values[51]. Gladstone senior was a major buyer of railway shares[52]. Charles Chetwynd-Talbot, the 2nd Earl of Talbot, owned Ingestre Hall and a grand Estate which borders the Haywoods. He received £4,660 (£3.4 million today) for the 543 slaves he had owned[53]. The ill-gotten cash no doubt came in handy when the family acquired Alton Towers, a few miles away. The delights of *Nemesis* and *Oblivion* at Britain's most-visited theme park cannot be blamed on the Talbots, however, as the building and grounds had been sold off in the early 20th century.

On the face of it, there was also opposition to the railways from some sections of the wealthy. Just as a noble Lord had opposed the construction of the Liverpool-Manchester line, objections from members of the landed classes would continue whenever railway developers wanted to cut through their estates. But often as not the objection would be a ruse to screw as much compensation from the railway company as possible[54] – and in this the large landowners were often supremely successful. Ludicrously large sums of money would be handed over for what at most would be narrow strips of cheap agricultural land[55]. These payments often amounted to a high proportion of the total capital outlay for a new railway. When the London & Birmingham and the Grand Junction companies between them effectively created a railway running all the way from London to the North-West, a fifth of their combined initial share capital was used to 'compensate' landowners[56]. Others benefitted quite handsomely, too. At the front of the queue would be the lawyers who drew up the legal agreements, only too happy to have found yet another lucrative fee-generator.

All this meant that 'free-market Britain' turned out to be a rather expensive place to build railways[57]. And, in addition to raking in the cash, landowners could sometimes negotiate route alterations or expensive engineering solutions to minimise any possible disturbance by a train passing within hearing distance of their stately homes. For example, Viscount Anson, the first Earl of Lichfield, protested that the proposed route of the Trent Valley railway would pass over his country estate at Shugborough within three-quarters of a mile of his bedroom. A successful claim for financial compensation was made for this devastating assault on his lordship's wellbeing. But in addition the Earl not only managed to persuade the company to hide much of the route through an immensely expensive 777 yard long tunnel, he also insisted that the tunnel entrances be in keeping with the ornately grand monuments on his estate. And perhaps the company would be good enough to throw in an ornamental bridge while they were at it[58]? The Viscount may have learnt his negotiating skills from his father who a generation earlier had managed to get the main Stafford to Lichfield road diverted further away 'to give him more privacy'[59].

The manor of Shugborough had been bought by barrister William Anson in 1624 and the family name has been associated with Shugborough ever since. Seventy years later his grandson, another William, had a replacement house built and it is this which forms the central part of today's Shugborough Hall. When Patrick Lichfield, the society photographer and cousin of one removal to the

Queen, became the 5th Earl in 1960, the Hall was transferred to the National Trust, in lieu of death duties. It is currently administered on behalf of the Trust by Staffordshire County Council. Set in 900 acres of stunning parkland and riverside gardens, Shugborough is now advertised as the country's *'only complete working historic estate'* and attracts a quarter of a million visitors a year[60].

Major additions to the house were made in the 1740s and soon after almost the entire village of Shugborough together with vast tracts of nearby Cannock Chase had come under Anson family control[61]. Keen to show off the impressive Hall to best effect, the family decided to establish the lands around the house as parkland. There was a problem, however. Shugborough Village, a settlement of 28 households, home to many of the estate workers, was considered something of an eyesore. So it was got rid of. By 1770, most of the village no longer existed although the last cottage was not demolished until the final tenant died in 1802. At last, the view from the big house was no longer interrupted. Some replacement housing for tenants and estate workers was built on the other side of the river in Great Haywood and Little Haywood but not, it seems from some accounts, until the existing houses had long since gone[62].

Even so, the transition of Shugborough village from existence to obliteration was at least gentler than elsewhere, where owners had other plans for their great estates. Advised that sheep would be economically more viable than people on her Scottish acres, the Duchess of Sutherland forcibly evicted thousands of peasants from their land and their homes.

> *'Between 1814 and 1820…15,000 inhabitants, about 3,000 families, were systematically hunted and rooted out. All their villages were destroyed and burnt, all their fields turned into pasturage. British soldiers enforced this mass of evictions, and came to blows with the inhabitants. One old woman was burnt to death in the flames of the hut she refused to leave. It was in this manner that this fine lady [the Duchess] appropriated 794,000 acres of land which had belonged to the clan from time immemorial.'*[63]

The removal of peasants from common land and from the open field system, and their replacement by sheep, started a long time before the Highland Clearances, however. Land enclosure, the practice of converting open land into patches of private property, had been going on since the late Middle Ages. Over a considerable period, changes in the forms of landownership were followed by changes in the organisation of agricultural production and in farming techniques. Some writers use the term agricultural revolution to refer to the times when these changes were most noticeable. They argue that the increases in agricultural productivity that resulted eventually allowed the industrial revolution to get underway in the mid-18th century. And it was about then that English agriculture started to experience a new, and final, wave of enclosures.

This time, the process of enclosing land did not so much involve the conversion of arable land to pasture as the reverse: the creation of more productive arable and mixed farming out of existing pasture land, open fields and wasteland[64]. Greater returns for landowners could now be made by producing food for the rapidly growing populations of the industrial towns. For the new band of industrialists in the towns, the enclosures would have the benefit of providing an additional pool of labour for their factories. The newly dispossessed 'surplus' of agricultural workers whose ancestors had lived from the land for centuries would now be 'free' to join the ranks of the industrial working classes, and many of them did. But there were periods when economic conditions slowed down the process of industrialisation. There was not always a sufficient number of jobs in manufacturing industry to offset work in the countryside, even if it was feasible to uproot one's entire family and find somewhere to live in a nearby town. At these times rural poverty was deep and extensive[65]. In the early decades of the 19th century, local ratepayers were complaining of the increasing expense of the existing system of poor relief. In response, the government brought in measures intended to reduce the cost but wrapped them in an ideology that claimed it was acting in the best interests of the poor themselves. Government excuses for reducing the number, scope and expense of welfare benefits in the years following the 2008 banking crisis showed striking similarities with those that accompanied the abolition, in 1834, of the old Poor Law and its replacement with a system based on the hated workhouse.

Over the centuries, the enclosure movements and the changes in land tenure that accompanied the breakdown of feudalism had produced a 'tripartite system' in the countryside. By the 19th century, a small class of *large landowners and gentry* owned 85% of the land in England. Each owner would divide most of their land into a series of holdings to be rented to *tenant farmers*. The landlords would typically provide the fixed capital – the farm houses, farm buildings and drainage; their tenants the working capital of livestock, carts and farm equipment[66]. In 1881, there were more than 230,000 farmers in England and Wales – one of whom was William Sproston at Navigation Farm. The tenanted farms would often be of a size where it was necessary to hire labour additional to that provided by the farmers and their families themselves[67]. Of the almost 900,000 *agricultural workers* recorded in 1881, a minority would be farm bailiffs or foremen or skilled farm craftsmen. Some of these would be hired for the year and receive board and lodging as part of their job. The majority, however, would be employed as agricultural labourers entirely dependent on their wage which was often paid by the day or at piece-rates[68].

For farmers, the new enclosures often worked more favourably where the latest agricultural inventions and best-practice farming methods were employed. In fact, it was often the farmers themselves who came up with the ideas for new farm machinery or making improvements in farm management. Designed to increase agricultural yields, and thereby income, such developments were also of economic interest to the landowners: financially successful farms would justify raising rents[69]. Thomas Coke, owner of a vast estate in Norfolk, for example, became famous for being an agricultural innovator and champion of progressive farming techniques. After his daughter, Ann, married Thomas Anson in 1806, it is thought that Coke's influence helped put Shugborough on the agricultural map[70]. A century earlier, the local villages were still untouched by enclosures or new farming techniques[71]. But from the late 1700s, the county of Staffordshire was becoming known for its leading role in agricultural development. And, together with a few other farms in the vicinity, Shugborough's Park Farm was to become one of the best-run agricultural setups in the country[72].

In addition to Shugborough itself, much of the farmland in and around Little Haywood and Colwich was owned by the Earls of Lichfield – including the fields adjacent to Park Farm that the Sproston family farmed. Not long after William became tenant of Navigation Farm, the downturn in agricultural fortunes known as the agricultural depression began. Although incomes from agricultural rents took quite a tumble, financial diversification and some sound management meant that, unlike some other large estates, Shugborough survived the depression largely intact[73]. William, and after his death a partnership of three of his sons, was able to continue farming parts of the vast acreage of lands that formed his lordship's estates.

A 1909 agreement between the Rt Hon Thomas Francis, third Earl of Lichfield (the landlord) and the brothers (the tenants), for example, shows James, Herbert and William (junior) Sproston renting almost 100 acres (22 acres arable, the rest pasture), as well as the Navigation Inn and outbuildings, at a rental of £202.15s for the year[74]. Most of the rented land lay between Seven Springs, an area of Cannock Chase just south of the River Trent, and the Knotty Line and the Inn, to the north of the canal. The fields lay on both sides of Meadow Lane but to the west they extended to where a bow in the river formed a boundary with Shugborough's own Park Farm. In addition to the rented land, however, it appears that the brothers also owned some land themselves. Attached to the rental agreement is a letter confirming a rent reduction in return for allowing his lordship 'sporting rights' over their land. Taken together, it would seem that the Sproston brothers worked most of the available farmland on the south side of the village. Although much of this land was liable to flooding, and to marauding bands of gun-toting Edwardian Hooray Henrys in pursuit of game, the water meadows of the Trent valley did, and still do, provide good grazing[75].

Together with the roads, canal and river, the two railway lines passing through Little Haywood provided the boundaries to some of the brothers' rented fields. The *Knotty* also demarcated the southern limit of Christopher's smallholding. Looking after his livestock next to the North Staffs Railway line, he would barely give a thought to the regularly passing trains. They had been a constant throughout his life, from the days when they passed within feet of his bedroom window as a child. The orgy of investment that had begun in the mid-1840s, and which had been responsible for both the village's railway lines, was over years before Christopher had been born.

The end of railway mania had been abrupt. In 1847, the value of railway shares crashed. Among the middle classes, bankruptcies mushroomed and debtors' prisons were filling up[76]. Some, including two of the Bronte sisters, merely got their fingers burned or their purses singed. The banking system was on the verge of collapse but was bailed out by the government pumping in public funds – perhaps as a practice-run for the much bigger publicly-financed gift to bankers 160 years later. The economic downturn of the late 1840s was not caused by the railway companies alone and, indeed, the optimistic activities of railway investors during the 'mania' had probably been covering up pre-existing fault lines in the economy. Yet the bubble of railway mania burst, in the words of Christian Wolmar, *'because ultimately it was based on little more than optimism feeding on itself'*[77].

There had been investment booms – and crashes – before (the South Sea Bubble of 1720 being one of the more notorious), but not on this scale. When the railway bubble burst, share value equivalent to half the national income had been lost[78]. People seemed genuinely surprised that the 'get rich quick, money-for-nothing' schemes offered by 'unscrupulous fraudsters'[79] and the railway companies alike helped to produce *'a financial panic and a national slump'*[80]. Booms and slumps have occurred a number of times since, of course. Perhaps the only surprising thing is that people are still surprised when they do happen.

By the time of the crash, railways had become a central and essential part of the nation's economy. The railway companies were by now large-scale businesses. The sheer amounts of capital raised for and invested in the industry (not that the two totals would be identical) dwarfed those in any other. Given the lack of regulation of the railway companies themselves and of the financial sector in general, it is no wonder that gullible investors would be parted from their money by legal as well as illegal means and that incompetence as well as corruption would be revealed when it all started to end in tears. And corruption and illegality were not in short supply. Historians such as Harold Perkin have described how *'the irresponsible power of these giant [railway] companies'* – and of the tycoons who headed them – was used against *'their customers, their employees and even the government'*[81].

The most powerful of the new-style business tycoons or 'railway barons' was George Hudson. A former mayor of York, Hudson became known as the 'Railway King' for his knack of buying up local railway companies on the cheap, amalgamating them into regional and economically more viable units, and then controlling them. And from 1845-1859, he was also Conservative MP for Sunderland. Like many business people who preach the supposed benefits of free-market, competitive capitalism, Hudson hated competition. When his railway interests were faced with honest rivalry, he was not averse to mounting 'secret dirty tricks' campaigns to discredit his competitors[82]. He was also a liar, cheat, insider-dealer, fraudster, embezzler, briber of MPs and all-round crook who was able to get away with his corrupt and illegal activities for so long by an enthusiastic adherence to the principles of the minimalist school of accountancy.

When Hudson's crimes eventually caught up with him, he fled into exile but was arrested and imprisoned on his return. His disgrace was confirmed when his waxwork at Madame Tussaud's was melted down. *George Hudson Street* in York was renamed *Railway Street*, but over a century later the good burghers of York decided to reinstate the original. His spell in prison was short and a whip-round from his remaining friends (together with Hudson's own determination to avoid paying off his debts) ensured that the rest of his life was spent in modest comfort[83]. He certainly did not have to endure the sort of poverty experienced by many in Victorian Britain, including no doubt some of those he had previously defrauded or exploited. In the small London house where he died, he probably spent his final days muttering to himself: 'I used to be a railway king, me.'

Despite the severity of the crash and the economic downturn

of the late 1840s, most of the railway companies survived[84], and many of the lines for which capital had been raised were built. The bursting of the railway mania bubble merely tempered, for a time, and certainly did not kill off further railway expansions. Working on the assumption that greed will triumph over experience, by the 1860s investors' wallets and purses were once again being purged by the combined laxative of an unregulated banking system and the railway companies' tempting prospectuses for yet further miles of railway – some of them overseas. And, of course, sooner or later the inevitable would happen. The bubble of this 'mini-mania' burst in 1866. This time it precipitated a credit crisis and what was then '*the worst banking collapse in British history*', leaving in its wake failed banks and the downfall of three big railway companies and many railway contractors[85].

Once a railway network has been established, however, its very interconnectedness and its infra-structural importance to the whole economy protects it from being returned to the soil and weeds from which it sprung. Just as would be said of the banking system a century and a half later (during an even greater financial crisis): it was too big to fail. So, the railways were kept running – but not without a panic gripping the entire industry. The situation looked so bad at one stage that, in the era of Victorian free-market capitalism, when any whiff of state intervention would normally produce a collective apoplexy, there was the delicious picture of a delegation of arch-Tory railway leaders petitioning a Tory Prime Minister in effect to nationalise the industry[86]. They did not get their way; presumably they were told to call back in 80 years and try again.

Before long, however, railway expansion was back on the agenda. And once again the inveterate and optimistic investor would ensure that there were times when the industry was over-capitalised. The result was that lines which never stood a chance of turning a profit continued to be built. Some did provide a socially useful function but others were just unnecessary duplications of existing lines[87]. The network continued to expand up to the start of the First World War when total mileage reached almost 24,000[88], although after 1870 much of the expansion was in branch-line development. There was traffic growth, too. The railway companies continued to increase their share of goods carriage relative to the canals and roads, and between 1870 and 1912 their passenger numbers quadrupled.

Any complacency that this escalation in custom may have engendered in the railway companies was dented from time to time by the issue of rail safety. In the spirit of 'free enterprise', Victorian governments allowed the companies to do much as they pleased. It is therefore hardly surprising that profit maximisation was their number one concern[89]. Safety came way down the list and railway accidents were fairly common in the early days. *Punch* magazine advised passengers to carry an emergency kit containing

> '*a small bottle of water, a tumbler, a complete set of surgical instruments, a packet of lint, and directions for making a will*'[90].

Safety tended to move up the agenda only after particularly horrendous accidents. And there were some spectacular examples during the height of the railway era. The collapse of the Tay Bridge in 1879 was responsible for the deaths of all 75 occupants of the train attempting to cross it – and for one of the worst poems ever written. Ten years later at Armagh a runaway train carrying mainly children resulted in 80 deaths and 250 injuries. A holiday train was derailed at Preston in 1896 and there was a major collision at Salisbury ten years later[91]. By far the biggest railway disaster in terms of loss of life, however, occurred at Quintinshill, north of Carlisle, in 1915. A horrifying collision, involving three trains, killed at least 227 people many of them soldiers of the Royal Scots regiment who had just finished their training and were on the first part of their journey to Gallipoli. Unlike the earlier disasters, wartime censorship meant that press coverage of the incident was muted[92].

For passengers, though, rail traffic, even in its worse days, has always been relatively safe – especially when compared with the roads. And this is still the case. The predominant form of transport of the late 19th century was a good deal safer than the predominant form of the 20th and 21st centuries. It is just that when a rail accident does occur it can involve a large number of casualties or otherwise be a particularly dramatic spectacle[93]. Such incidences have not passed the villages by. Colwich Junction was the site of a major rail crash in 1986. Two packed inter-city passenger trains collided, both locomotives were derailed and overturned as were several carriages. Seventy-five of the almost 900 passengers were injured but there were no deaths. The driver of one of the trains, however, was killed as his engine ploughed into the other at 100 mph[94].

Indeed, for those working on the railways, the safety story has always been rather different. Employees have accounted for a much greater proportion of railway deaths than customers. In terms of the number of accidents, during the 19th century the railway industry was the third most dangerous to work in – after coal mining and the merchant navy[95]. For decades it was rare for railway workers or their families to receive any compensation for injury or death, the assumption being that work accidents were the fault of the worker[96].

The railways were a big employer of labour: the industry had a total permanent workforce of 620,000 by the end of the 19th century, increasing to 650,000 by 1914 – in skilled and unskilled manual and non-manual jobs[97]. In the 19th century it was an almost exclusively male industry. The employment of women increased in the 20th century and, as was the case in other critical industries, during the two world wars women took on many of the jobs previously done by men. In both cases, however, only a minority of the women remained for long in 'male-graded' posts after the cessation of hostilities. Although the numbers were somewhat higher after the Second World War, the pre-war attitudes towards women working in traditionally-regarded 'male' jobs had been quick to return[98].

In the Victorian era huge bureaucratic organisations ran most of the railways, often on quasi-military lines. They were the prototypes of the vast modern corporations[99] that would come to dominate the business world internationally. In the early years, it could be a reasonably attractive industry to work in: higher rates of pay and a degree of security were offered by some companies. But trade unions were effectively kept out of the industry until the 1870s and full collective bargaining was not established until the First World War[100]. Consequently, pay levels started to lag behind those in other industries and very long hours were demanded of the workers. Shifts of 16-18 hours, six days a week were not uncommon, and this increased the risk of accidents to both staff and passengers. Recruits were still being attracted by what appeared to be greater job security, compared with other industries of the period, even though instant dismissal was by no means unknown[101].

Once they had gained a foothold within the industry, trade unions did manage to challenge some of the military-style discipline and management practices that were being seen as increasingly out-of-date. Even so, it was not until 1911 that the first national railway strike was called. Railworkers had become tired of seeing a relative decline in their wage levels whilst rail company dividends paid to shareholders were increasing. Fearing the knock-on effects of the industrial action on the rest of the economy, Home Secretary Winston Churchill ordered the mobilisation of 58,000 troops to help defend the railway companies. In Llanelli, two people died when soldiers opened fire after strikers had stopped a train[102]. Further developments over the following couple of years saw the amalgamation of three of the unions. But before the new found strength could be properly tested, an industrial truce was agreed at the outbreak of the First World War[103].

When the war started, the railways had been in existence for more than 80 years. Just as Britain had benefitted in the earlier stages of the industrial revolution from the profits of slavery, the early days of railway development saw substantial sums invested from the compensation given after slavery's abolition. But this was by no means the only source of cash sloshing about the railway investment trough, particularly during the railway mania and the other occasions of frenzied financial activity. Over the period of their development, the railways had changed the face of the country even more than the canals had done. Although they did not immediately make the canal network redundant, the railways did show major advantages. It was not subject to delays caused by frost, drought or flood to anywhere near the same degree as canals (reports of leaves on the line or the wrong type of snow did not seem to feature in the early days). The railways were generally more reliable and they were much faster than the transport on either the canals or the roads. By the end of the 19th century, canals were carrying only a tenth of the tonnage of the railways[104] and the heyday of the roads still lay in the future.

The Navigation Inn had begun life with and because of the

canals. With the advent of the Knotty Line, essential deliveries to the Inn now came by rail. By the time William had moved there, beer barrels were shunted from the station at Colwich then rolled down the embankment to the pub cellar[105]. In Little Haywood, the Trent & Mersey Canal had had a lasting impact on the community. The Trent Valley and the North Staffs railways had now left their own marks. Between them, the canal and the two sets of lines physically demarcated the working practices and movements of the Sprostons, especially those engaged directly in farming.

As well as running the farm in the early years of the 20th century, the partnership of three Sproston brothers, Nel's uncles, continued to operate their late father's coal business. But by 1911 things seem to have changed[106]. William is no longer listed as a partner in the businesses – describing himself in the 1911 census as a wagoner. Herbert, now a widower and living with his older brother's family at Navigation Inn, is recorded as a co-worker. In the following year's trade directory, of the three former fraternal business partners only James gets a mention under Little Haywood (at the Navigation Inn) but the 'Sproston Brothers' are recorded as farmers at *Great* Haywood[107]. It seems that no longer holding the tenancy to the Little Haywood farmland, they may by now have been farming only their own land. By that time, four of James's sons were assisting him as farm workers and a daughter was employed as a 'domestic' at the family home[108]. And with the closure of the pub in 1912, it is possible that the businesses could no longer support three chiefs and their families. By 1916, James, too, has disappeared from the business listings. He died thirteen years later, leaving an estate worth £141 – considerably less than that left by his father and stepmother[109].

In 1916, brother Albert is included as a farmer in Colwich, having passed the reins of the Post Office to a relative of his stepmother[110]. But the only remaining trade listing for a Sproston in Little Haywood is now Christopher the 'cowkeeper'. Christopher and Ellen remained in the village, continuing to live at Ivy Cottage, until their deaths in the years following the Second World War. Christopher was the first to go but not before he and Ellen had received a message of congratulation from King George VI on New Year's Eve, 1947. This was the day they celebrated their diamond wedding anniversary. Four months later, Christopher's life came to an end, at home – exactly one hundred years after his grandfather Thomas's exit just a couple of miles away at Shirleywich. He was 84. Christopher became the first Haywood Sproston to spend his entire life in the same village. Indeed, probably not since the pre-Job days in Middlewich had an adult in the direct Sproston line died in the place where he was born.

Half a century earlier, though, Ellen was newly pregnant with her seventh and final child. In June 1904, Morris Bernard (always known by his second name) joined his older siblings: Irene May (Rene) not yet two years old, Albert Edward aged five, William James (Bill) who was seven, the 11-year-old twins John Colin (Jack) and Eleanor Mary (Nel) and, the eldest, Christopher (Hazel), now 13.

Given her age, and as the elder girl, Nel would have been expected to share with her mother the responsibility for looking

Ellen (with baby Rene) and Christopher Sproston, with Hazel, Nel, Jack, Bill and Albert – in front of their Coley Lane house c.1902, shortly before the move to Ivy Cottage. [Courtesy of Colin Sproston]

after the new baby. She had probably already been doing the same for her young sister, Rene, and perhaps for her younger brothers, too. But the burden would have been eased somewhat by the very close relationship that existed between Nel and her twin brother, Jack.

Chapter 7

... and Nel

Nel and Jack Sproston celebrated their eighth birthdays on 22 January 1901. It was also the day that the Victorian age officially came to an end. The monarch who had reigned over Britain and its empire for 63 years, and whose name defines a momentous historical era, was dead. And perhaps nothing encapsulates the era so well and so graphically as the railways.

The twins: Nel and Jack

When Victoria became Queen in 1837, the landscape of the Haywoods and Colwich was still unscarred by the revolutionary new form of transport. A few miles away, however, the first railway line to pass through Staffordshire, and the country's first major trunk line, was just about to open. By the time of her death, it had become difficult to imagine life without the railways. They had altered the layout of the villages. They had changed the face of Britain. As one writer has put it, the railways linked

> *'the country to the town, the towns to one another and inland industrial regions to the sea, in an entirely new system of communications.'*[1]

In fact, some historians like to refer to the 30 or 40 years before the First World War as the 'great' or 'golden' age of the railways in Britain[2]. Rail transport had by then clearly proved itself against the canals. It was not yet under much threat from the motor vehicle and even less from the still experimental aeroplane. At an industry-wide level, therefore, the railways were now in a virtual monopoly position. Internationally, British railway hardware, engineering know-how and the technical experience of its skilled labour force were much in demand.

But there are also doubts about whether a golden age ever existed. In the year Queen Victoria died, *The Times* newspaper was warning of the dangers of Britain's railway companies importing locomotives from the USA in preference to home-built engines[3]. The period was also one when the railway companies were subjected to almost constant criticism for the arrogant disregard shown to their customers and to their employees[4]. The lack of concern for people or things other than shareholder profits is likely to reach its peak in any industry that enjoys a monopolistic position and yet remains largely unregulated, so there are no proper checks on the policies or actions of the companies involved. In non-essential industries this would be frustrating or annoying. In an industry that had become crucial to the workings of the economy and society, it was a major issue. And, indeed, it would be hard to overestimate just how important the railways were to the economic and social life of Britain.

For a start, the railway industry itself impacted directly on the economy. The materials and skills needed for the construction and operation of the railways meant that the demand for coal, iron, bricks (think of all the bridges, the tunnels, the stations), and the products of mechanical engineering (locomotives, rolling stock, signalling equipment, automatic brakes, and so on) either vastly increased or gave birth to entirely new industries[5]. Even before the first half of the 19th century was over, the railways were one of the largest employers of labour and users of capital. In creating employment and generating flows of wages all over the country, the economy was stimulated in countless ways nationally and locally[6].

By the end of the century, practically all branches of the economy had expanded because of the railways. The movement of goods across the entire range of British industry had not only been significantly accelerated, new markets – in this country and beyond – had been opened up.

The railways were responsible for the emergence of the modern form of business organisation. For a time some of the railway enterprises in Britain were the largest commercial companies in the world and the London & North Western Railway Company, which swallowed up the Trent Valley Company, was the largest of all[7]. Through its pioneering of big-business and use of the joint-stock company device for raising capital, the railway industry had shifted capitalism onto a much larger scale than that known to the owner-managers of the mills and factories of the early stages of the industrial revolution[8]. It also produced a rapidly growing professional class of lawyers, accountants and managers to keep these organisations functioning on a daily basis.

Business could now be carried out at a faster pace because of the *'increase in human mobility'* which the railways had made possible[9]. This in part is what Sydney Smith seemingly had in mind in 1842. Perhaps anticipating the globalisation debate of the late 20th century, whilst perpetuating stereotypes of the Scot, he wrote:

'Railroad travelling is a delightful improvement of human life. Man is become a bird... The early Scotchman scratches himself in the morning mists of the North; and has his porridge in Piccadilly before

*the setting of the sun… Everything is near, everything is immediate –
time, distance, and delay are abolished.'[10]*

But it was not only in the direct movement of people that communications were expedited. The geographical distribution of newspapers was speeded up and postal and telegraphic services greatly expanded through the railways[11]. Animals and animal products could be moved more quickly and cost-effectively over greater distances.

Initially, most farmers benefitted from this speedy access to wider markets. But towards the end of the century wheat and livestock farmers were complaining of cheap imports from the Americas. They also disliked the preferential rates that British railway companies sometimes gave to these imported agricultural products[12]. The dairy-farming Sprostons, however, were not directly affected by this overseas competition. Even in the years of agricultural depression, milk sales nationally were holding up well, as the fast rail transport had extended travel distance and thereby opened up new markets in Britain's growing urban areas[13].

Ironically, it was British engineering skills and labour, as well as capital, which had helped develop the rail networks across the prairies of North and South America, allowing these vast continents to produce and transport foodstuffs for export[14]. During the Victorian era and up to the First World War, Britain's balance of payments benefitted tremendously from the export of rails, locomotives, rolling-stock and signalling equipment – as well as the technical expertise of railway engineers and skilled labour. Britain's overseas investments and credit stood at £110 million at the start of the railway age in 1830 and rose to £4,000 million by 1914. As Harold Perkin has noted, half of this was then blown on the First World War and the other half spent on the Second[15].

Overall, in the 70 years between the opening of the Liverpool & Manchester line and the end of the 19th century, industrial production increased six-fold and the railways could justifiably claim credit for a big chunk of this. In the second half of the century, national income per head more than doubled in real terms[16]. This did not mean, of course, that everyone in the country became twice as well off. The vast inequalities of income (and of wealth, as well) was a feature of the times – as indeed it is in early 21st century Britain.

Inequalities of income and wealth are indicators of a class society and the railways had a somewhat contradictory part to play in both reflecting and changing the nature of some of Britain's class relationships. For some 19th century observers, the railway was 'democratising' travel and thereby helping to reduce class divisions[17]. Yet the early adoption of first, second and third class rail travel seemed only to confirm the particular three-class model of society that was becoming entrenched in Victorian minds and society. The distinctions even extended to the conveyance of dead bodies. An enterprising businessman created a vast cemetery 25 miles from London to ease graveyard overcrowding in the capital, and arranged for special trains to run from Waterloo. Not only did the 'stiffs express' contain separate carriages for the three classes of mourners, the corpses were similarly segregated[18].

Besides, in the early days, trains were patronised primarily by the middle and upper classes, even after a legal requirement of 1844 that each line should provide at least one cheap service per day. When poorer passengers did use the new form of transport, they were initially carried in open or windowless freight trucks[19]. Some rail companies, however, began to see the potential for catering for mass travel, whether by special workmen's trains[20] or in providing holiday excursions. For the first time, travel became a real possibility for the working class.

Before the opening of Colwich station in 1847, only the wealthier local residents – and a few of their servants – would be likely to have experienced life outside the county of Staffordshire. In the course of their work, some others would have made infrequent if regular trips to Rugeley, the nearest market town. A few may have spent the odd wild away-day in Stafford, Stone or Lichfield. But there would have been many in the villages who had never ventured beyond the parish boundaries. There would have been no need to. Until Christopher, the line of boatmen meant that the core Sproston family had been a rare exception to this geographical immobility[21]. The railway would make many more exceptions so that all but the poorest or most infirm villager would experience the delights of travel. For some, it would become a necessity, providing transport to work. The first train to leave Colwich each day was the 5.45 am, scheduled to get coal miners to the pits in the Rugeley area for the start of their shifts, for example[22].

But there was another, less direct, way by which the new mode of transport may have helped to shape the developing class relations of the 19th century. Highlighted by the railway mania of the mid-1840s, the railways triggered major changes to the form and extent of capital investment. Gambling on the prospects of future business performance had spread to larger numbers of people and the joint stock company was the future card game of choice. It confirmed that, economically at least, Britain had become a bourgeois society. It was the new and capitalist middle class that had by now replaced the old landed aristocracy as the dominant class. In the words of Harold Perkin, it was now this class that could:

'impose its beliefs in free trade, competitive individualism, laissez-faire, the gospel of work and [its] puritan morality ... upon the rest of society.'[23]

Other features and developments of Victorian society can also be attributed wholly or in part to the railways. The giant clock became a feature of Victorian rail stations, for example. Accurate timing is of course essential to the operational planning and execution of a national rail system. Variable times or different time zones across the country would make such planning difficult and travel hazardous. So it was the railways that were responsible for the introduction of a standard time (Greenwich Mean Time) throughout the country and, in 1884, the establishment internationally of Greenwich as the international zero meridian[24].

The opening up of national markets for fresh foodstuffs – vegetables, fruit, fish and milk – may not have guaranteed everyone getting their five-a-day, but the general impact on most people's diet was a positive one. More people were eating better. And, because of the railway, fish and chip shops were no longer the sole preserve of the seaside towns[25]. A national dish emerged.

Over the countryside and in town, 19th century railway architecture was leaving its distinctive signatures on the national scenery through the stations, the bridges and viaducts, the tunnel entrances, even the signal boxes. To make way for these new structures, and for the mile upon mile of track that carved its unforgiving way through densely populated areas, hundreds of thousands of poorer people were made homeless as their rented accommodation was flattened. Unlike the landed classes they received no compensation[26].

Even those fortunate enough to retain a roof over their heads would not necessarily escape the direct consequences of the railway on where they would live. New residential centres quickly developed around the vast workshops needed to build or maintain the locomotives, the carriages, and so on. Swindon and Crewe, for example, virtually became company towns and had barely existed as communities before the railways[27]. Elsewhere, the railways were directly responsible for the phenomena of suburbia and commuter traffic and were influential in the development of new types of housing estates. Probably their main contribution, however, was to accelerate urbanisation – a process which had begun with the application of steam power in the pre-railway era. Half of Britain's population was living in towns and cities in 1851; just 40 years later it was almost three-quarters[28].

The various forms of the transport revolution had helped define the contours of village life in Little Haywood and those of its neighbours. Where routed through existing urban areas, though, the railways impacted heavily and immediately on much greater numbers of people. Slicing through already established districts of high population density, the railways almost overnight created new social zones and gave rise to the expression 'the wrong side of the tracks'[29]. They were often significant in demarcating the highly class-segregated housing areas which became such a feature of British towns and cities[30].

In the second half of the 19th century, the railways made it possible for the wealthy classes to move some distance away from the towns and cities which the sources of their wealth – their factories and other places of industry – had made overcrowded, dirty and smelly.

Before then, the most they could do was ensure that housing for their workers was confined to the east side of town while building their own impressive residences on the west side to offer some protection from the prevailing winds which carried the smoke and pollutants and smells in the opposite direction. With the coming of the suburban railways, the wealthy could leave the towns altogether and live in the country or by the sea. In addition to the railways, horse-drawn buses and trams started to provide more localised forms of transport. As a result, the built-up areas themselves were being divided even more finely into distinct housing class areas based on social status and rental amounts[31].

By the turn of the century, then, some of Britain's largest cities and towns had been suburbanised. A typical pattern, moving from the centre, would be something like this: an inner core of shops, offices and warehouses; beyond this the factories, mills, and railway yards together with the worst of the slums; then a broader ring of row after row of graded terraced housing for the working classes, followed by an outer ring of lower-middle and middle class estates; and finally the railway suburbs – not in a circle but *'strung like beads along the railway lines'*, each a self-contained village with its own station[32]. Even these would be socially and economically graded, though, with the grandest residences the farthest away from the city.

The motor vehicle of the 20th century would allow many of the gaps between the village stations to be infilled with newer housing[33]. But even then, with road transport in the ascendancy, railway-generated suburbs continued, the most notable example being the development of 'Metro-land' to the north-west of London in the 1920s and 1930s.

The increasing class-segregation of society, facilitated by the railway, may have helped the development of a greater political awareness in the working class areas of the towns. Furthermore, the railways had already made it easier for working class movements such as Chartism and trade unionism to develop on a national scale – but also easier for the authorities to control them[34]. Some historians believe that railway mania spared Britain the revolutionary activity seen on the continent in the late 1840s. According to this argument, discontent following the financial crash was absorbed by all the opportunities for employment in railway construction that the wild investment had made possible[35]. On the more mundane level of party political campaigning, the railways enabled a new dimension that was to last for well over a century. Leading politicians could now travel all over the country to address large political gatherings[36].

Overall, those 19th century optimists who believed the railways would be great social levellers would be disappointed. There is one area, though, where the railways did go some way in opening up society: leisure. By the second half of the 19th century, day trips and excursions with cheap fares were encouraging the working classes to explore beyond their own doorsteps[37]. Existing seaside holiday places, such as Blackpool, Brighton and Scarborough – once largely the playgrounds of the rich – became places of mass entertainment. And new ones developed, including the string of resorts along the North Wales coast[38]. Without the railways, people all over the country would not have been able to read a national daily newspaper within hours of its printing. Book sales took off when W H Smith started to sell cheap editions from station platforms.

Railways made possible the birth of national sports competitions and leagues, including county cricket and professional football. It was not only the supporters who could now travel to matches but (in the pre-Maserati and Bentley Continental days) the players, too. Until the 1960s even the country's top footballers were on a maximum weekly wage – often better than, but still on the same planet as, that earned by other working people. And fans could still watch their team each week without taking out a second mortgage. Thousands of spectators attended race meetings after stations were built next to courses (horses could be transported, too)[39].

The railways, then, helped to extend the concept of organised leisure activities far beyond the preserve of a wealthy, and often idle, few. Perhaps the railways also have things to answer for: not least the seemingly pointless, if harmless, pastime of trainspotting (although it was not until after the Second World War that it developed[40]).

Throughout much of pre-World War I British railway history, there was a trend within the industry for amalgamation and consolidation as the ever-larger companies sought the benefits of monopoly or near-monopoly situations within their regions. By the outbreak of war in 1914, the process had gone so far that meaningful competition had all but ceased. A few of the smaller companies managed to survive as successful and independent companies until the government brought in a major change in the early 1920s. One of these was the North Staffordshire Railway, the Knotty, whose trains continued to operate busily on just 112 miles of track in and around the Potteries and as far south as Colwich[41].

For the period of the First World War and its immediate aftermath, the government effectively took over the direction of the railways. In 1921 it rejected calls for nationalisation but nonetheless secured parliamentary approval to reduce the ownership and control of the 120 existing railway companies to just four regional conglomerates[42]. Coming into operation in 1923, the legislation also gave the government control over the fares that could be charged. This reduced room for manoeuvre, combined with a lack of funds to rebuild the railway system, meant the companies were less able to fend off the growing competition from motorised road transport[43].

What had largely been dismissed as an insignificant threat before the war, had, by the late 1930s become the single most important factor in the decline of the railways. By 1938, there were 1.8 million cars and almost half-a-million lorries on Britain's roads[44], a combined total six or seven times higher than 20 years earlier. Compared with the immediate pre-war period, the main rail lines had lost half their traffic. Although the railways were still by far the largest conveyor of freight, by 1939 road passengers were outnumbering rail by nearly 4:1.

Locally, the railways continued to provide employment for some residents of the villages – at least until the closure of both Colwich and Great Haywood stations in the late 1950s[45]. As well as reflecting railway decline, the closing of the latter was also indicative of the continuing diminution in influence of the aristocracy. The halt at Great Haywood had been built in the 19th century to serve the needs of the Ansons of Shugborough Hall. With just 24 hours' notice, trains could be ordered to make unscheduled stops there, should his lordship or a member of his family require such transport[46].

But it was not only the railway that would be viewed by the

family as existing primarily for its own convenience. The entire village would at one time have been seen in this light. Because of its historical connections to the local aristocratic piles of the Earls of Lichfield at Shugborough and, to a lesser extent, the Earls of Shrewsbury at nearby Ingestre, Great Haywood is described as having the *'character of an estate village'*[47]. For a long time it was virtually a self-sufficient, 'closed' community which could boast a wide variety of crafts and trades and had many small shops[48]. The village even had its own resident doctor. For part of the 19th century, this was a Dr Edward Tylecote who attained a degree of fame following the execution in 1856 of William Palmer, the notorious 'Rugeley Poisoner'. Palmer had been apprenticed to him ten years earlier and worked in the village as the doctor's assistant[49].

The Shugborough-Great Haywood connection is noticeable in some of the village architecture. Trent Lane, which leads from the centre of the village to Essex Bridge, is one of the small developments which eventually housed some of the estate workers after the destruction of Shugborough Village. The architectural historian and guide Nikolaus Pevsner referred to the lane as *'an anticipation of Shugborough'*[50] because the classical pillars and arches at the north end of the short row of cottages *'echo'* the Hall itself[51]. According to the local parish Village Design Statement, the same can be said of the adjacent railway bridge, carrying the Knotty line, which is *'built in matching classical style to form an arched entrance to Shugborough Park'*[51]. Indeed, as the local Conservation Area Document remarks:

> *'...much of the same character pervades both Shugborough and Great Haywood, different in scale and function but possessing an overall unity and a reminder of the life and purpose of a past age.'*[52]

Also built to house workers from the Shugborough estate was The Ring. The Ring was a unique construction of continuous terraced housing built in an octagon. Each house had its own garden but in the centre were communal facilities – such as a well, washhouse, bakehouse, fuel store and even a schoolroom – approached through an archway. For a time in the early 1900s, Number 14 was occupied by Frances Sproston, younger brother of William and uncle to Christopher. The development was demolished in the 1960s and replaced by bungalows[53].

The closing of the local stations foreshadowed the severe cuts that were made to the national rail network in the 1960s when more than 2,000 stations closed. The villages had come to rely on the railways as a source of employment. Nel's brother-in-law worked at Colwich Station and, when father Christopher's businesses began to taper off in the 1940s, brother Albert also took a rail job. The junction of the two lines and the building of the station a hundred years earlier had led directly to other buildings in Colwich which still survive, such as the row of red-brick railway cottages. The railway station no longer exists but the old *'strikingly Victorian'* Station House, *'with its Dutch gables and finials and tall chimney stacks'* is now a listed building[54].

Also listed are the nearby buildings of the old school and school house – *'red brick with stone dressings'*[55] – situated opposite the church. Although since extended, the school still exists and part of it is today a primary school for about 150 pupils from Colwich and Little Haywood. Another part of the old school buildings was later to be used as a Youth Centre where Nel's son-in-law was employed as Youth Leader in the 1960s and 1970s.

By the time Nel and Jack were ready to begin their formal education, school attendance in England and Wales had been a legal requirement for only 15 or so years. And it was not long before then that many children received no formal schooling at all. Up to the 1870s, it was very much a matter of what today would be called a postcode lottery: whether or not you attended school depended on where you lived. Nel's father, Christopher, and his brothers and sisters were fortunate to have lived in villages that had schools decades before anything approaching a national system of education existed. Unlike their father William, who grew up illiterate, they all learned to read and write and do sums. The children of boatpeople typically did not attend school or did so rarely. Attendance was more likely if families also had a place to live 'on land' – as did William's family from when they moved to Pasturefields – but even then once children reached the age of eight or nine they would often leave to work on the boats[56]. William and Elizabeth 1, however, seem to have been determined that their children would have more schooling than this. Their children attended schools between the ages of four and ten[57].

Before a change in the law in 1870, there had been no attempt to set up a national system of education in England and Wales. The inappropriately named 'public schools' for the sons of the very rich or well-connected (daughters would be educated, if at all, by private governesses at home) had been around for a long time. So, too, had some of the grammar schools and these, together with a variety of private schools, were favoured by the comfortably-off middle classes. Any form of secondary schooling, however, was out of the question for the vast majority of the population and many children were denied even a basic or elementary education.

Elementary schooling for working class children did exist, but provision was patchy. The main providers were the 'voluntary' bodies – the churches and other charities. Some towns and villages were well served, others had no school at all or offered only a limited number of places. From the late 1820s, boys from Colwich, Little Haywood and some of the surrounding villages benefitted from free schooling paid for by Charlotte Sparrow. The daughter of a wealthy banker from nearby Bishton Hall, Miss Sparrow founded a Church of England school in Colwich, agreeing to fund 170 pupil places. It was not until 1860, however, that girls were permitted to enrol. The founder is officially remembered each year when pupils lay posies on Charlotte Sparrow's grave in Colwich churchyard[58].

There is evidence that elsewhere in the village, and on a smaller scale, a 'poor school' was opened in the late-1830s. It seems that between 30 and 40 local children attended a day school, for which no fees were charged, under the instruction of a couple of nuns. Expelled from France during the Revolution, a Benedictine Order of nuns came to England, eventually settling in Colwich in what previously had been an aristocratic hunting lodge[59]. The order is still in residence in the same building today – it is now known as St Mary's Abbey – but the school lasted only a few years. It was deemed incompatible with the closed nature of the religious order[60]. The order is still a closed one; it does have a website but it is non-interactive[61].

In the 19th century, two schools were also built at Great Haywood, attached to the local churches of St John's (Roman Catholic) and St. Stephen's (Church of England). Nationally, the Anglican Church was the largest provider of elementary schools. Given the prevailing laissez-faire philosophy, it was not thought appropriate for the state itself to provide them. Besides, among sections of the ruling classes, there was no desire to widen access to education. Aware of the revolutionary activities taking place in France and Germany, they feared that an educated populace in this country might turn to subversion through their ability to read inflammatory literature. Similarly, it was felt that educating the masses would give them 'ideas above their station', making them discontented and thereby a threat to social order. Addressing the House of Commons in 1807, one MP declared that providing education for the working classes would encourage them:

> '... to despise their lot in life instead of making them good servants in agriculture and other laborious employments to which their rank in society [has] destined them. Instead of teaching them subordination, it will render them factious and refractory [and] insolent to their superiors. It will enable them to read seditious pamphlets, vicious books, and publications against Christianity.'[62]

From the 1830s, however, British governments began to assist the voluntary schools financially. The total amounts involved increased each year and, over the decades, pressure built for the state itself to become more directly involved in the provision of elementary education. It was argued that the churches were either unwilling or ill-equipped to provide the degree of educational expansion required in an industrialised society. Nothing short of at least a basic education for all children was being suggested.

As the 19th century progressed, the fear grew that Britain's economic predominance was being threatened by foreign competition, especially from Germany. From as early as the 1820s, some industrialists and politicians had been pointing to the superior German system of education and to the deficiencies in English schools to explain why the country was succumbing too easily to this threat[63]. By the 1860s, these and other concerns had coalesced into demands for a universal state system of basic education, although the arguments supporting this move varied. Some continued to emphasise the needs of an industrialised economy for a numerate and literate workforce. Many of the jobs involved in building, maintaining and operating the increasingly sophisticated railway network, for example, would have required such skills. In 1867, the right to vote in parliamentary elections had been extended to sections of the working class in urban areas, and some politicians argued that a basic education would ensure that future voters could at least read and be able to use their vote sensibly. Others took this further, suggesting that education might help to prevent political unrest. The belief here was that a universal system of education could act as a mechanism of social control. Most politicians probably saw an extension of educational provision as a way of perpetuating and reinforcing the existing class system, with one MP declaring:

'The lower classes ought to be educated to discharge the duties cast upon them. They should also be educated that they may appreciate and defer to a higher cultivation when they meet it, and the higher classes ought to be educated in a very different manner, in order that they may exhibit to the lower classes that higher education to which, if it were shown to them, they would bow down and defer.'[64]

Eventually Parliament approved legislation to ensure that in each district a 'sufficient' number of school places was provided. The 1870 Education Act declared that where no voluntary schools already existed, or where there was a shortage of places, a local school board would be elected to make up the deficiency. The boards would be able to build schools, funded by the state, and to raise a local rate (an earlier form of council tax) to help pay to run them. On introducing the Bill to Parliament, W E Forster, the government minister responsible, was keen to reassure the churches that the idea was to supplement, not to replace, their schools. At the same time, though, he wanted to emphasise the importance of the proposals when he declared:

'Upon [a] speedy provision of elementary education depends our industrial prosperity [and] our national power'[65].

The 1870s, therefore, represent the beginnings of a national system of elementary education for England and Wales. It was the start of the dual system of state schools and voluntary (primarily church) schools some semblance of which survives today. This dual system was a compromise, a way out of an impasse which had delayed the introduction of a national education system for so long. The biggest stumbling block to the state provision of schools had been the religious organisations themselves. They jealously guarded their role in providing education and did not want the state muscling in. In addition, supporters of the Church of England were opposed to spending local taxes on any schools that did not teach the Anglican version of Christianity. At the same time, the Nonconformists (the Methodists, Baptists, Presbyterians, and so on) were concerned that the introduction of state schools would further increase the influence and power of the Anglicans. They feared that the teachings of the Church of England, as the nation's Established Church, would be the version that such schools would adopt.

The resentment of the religious organisations continued even after the 1870 Act was passed. Over the next ten years, in a bid to retain their monopoly position of educational provision, they almost doubled the number of denominational schools[66] – a feat they had somehow been unable to achieve before the Act. Twenty-five years after the first state schools were built, more children were still attending the 'voluntary' schools than the state-run alternatives[67]. At a local level, church school supporters often went to great lengths to prevent the setting up of school boards[68]. And where boards were established they were sometimes hijacked by church members in an attempt to slow down the provision of board schools and to hamper their successful development.

In the run-up to the 1870 Act, educational reformers had put a strong case for school attendance to be made compulsory. This was necessary, they argued, to overcome the reluctance of those parents who saw little need for their children to be schooled. Their arguments, however, conflicted with middle-class beliefs about individual liberty prevalent in Victorian England[69]. It was felt that legal compulsion of school attendance would be an unreasonable interference with the rights and authority of the parent over the child. An initial proposal for national direct compulsion to be included in the legislation was therefore dropped. The 1870 Act did, however, allow each school board to set its own rules on attendance – within certain limits. And some boards took advantage of this to make school attendance compulsory within their areas – much to the displeasure of at least one member of the land-owning aristocracy:

> 'Since the present educational system has come into operation, the weeds have very much multiplied in Norfolk…, weeding being particularly the work of children whose labour is cheap, whose sight is keen, bodies flexible and fingers nimble.'[70]

But the pressures for universal compulsion did not go away. By 1876 about half of the country had some compulsory element attached to school attendance, although the proportion was considerably lower in rural areas where the Boards were weaker[71]. In 1880, though, compulsory attendance on a national basis was brought in (for 5-10 year olds). Support had come from business leaders and industrialists. They wanted the schools to instil values of discipline and obedience into their charges in order to produce future generations of conforming and compliant workers for their factories. National and local government bodies were also fretting about a breakdown of law and order within local communities. Wars and acts of terrorism aside, few things worry governments more than gangs of young people roaming about with apparently nothing to do. Following a series of Factory Acts from the 1830s onwards, child labour had progressively been outlawed from the country's factories. While their parents were still working long hours in the mills and on the shop floors, children were let loose every day onto the streets of Britain's towns and cities. The historian David Landes has claimed:

> '…whatever the ostensible aims of the supporters of compulsory elementary education, its essential function … was to discipline a

growing mass of disaffected proletarians and integrate them into British society. Its object was to civilise the barbarians.'[72]

Judging by comments of the early 1880s, it seemed to have the desired effect, to the satisfaction of the authorities and business owners alike:

'Since the passing of the Education Act more than one thousand Board School boys have found employment in [our] Cornwall works, and ... there is a most marked improvement in every way. The lads are more orderly, more amenable to discipline'[73].

And Her Majesty's Inspector for London wrote:

'... if it were not for her 500 elementary schools London would be overrun by a horde of young savages'[74]

Even so, it is one thing to legislate for compulsory school attendance, another to enforce it. Two years after national compulsion was introduced, less than two-thirds of children whose names appeared on school registers were attending regularly. Truancy was not only seen as a problem in the more socially anonymous urban areas. The long summer school holidays in England and Wales are a legacy of the agricultural requirement for children to work in the fields during the busy harvest periods. Despite this, it was still common for farm children to be kept away from school if they were needed to help out at other times. Even years after the introduction of compulsory school attendance, parental collusion in unauthorised absences for other reasons was still taking place. In 1907, the head teacher of Colwich School was 'disappointed' to note that 23 of his pupils did not attend the afternoon session on the day of the annual pleasure fair in Rugeley.

'...nearly all those who stayed away were the children of farmers who took them to Rugeley in carts after dinner.'[75]

A year later, the holding of a nearby fete produced a declaration from the same exasperated head teacher that *'attendance is simply ruined'*. It seems that on occasions skipping school could even have the tacit support of the local aristocracy – if it suited their purposes to hire the children for beating at Shugborough game shoots[76].

Nonetheless, after 1880, sufficient numbers of children were attending school regularly for the government to consider it worthwhile to raise the minimum school leaving age. By the end of the century, children of Nel's generation were expected to stay in education until they were 12 years old. At the end of the First World War, this was raised again to 14[77].

Despite the imposition of compulsory attendance – in some areas from 1870 – elementary education was not provided free at the point of use. Parents were expected to pay weekly fees, as prescribed by each school board. In some districts, the fees were as little as one (old) penny per pupil per week, but over the course of a year this could amount to a tidy sum for a large family on a restricted income[78]. A board could waive fees, wholly or partially, in cases of extreme poverty, but the prevailing attitude was still that parents should make some contribution towards their children's education in case they *'should become feckless, …fail in their duty [and] not appreciate the value of education'*[79]. *The Times* newspaper went so far as to label even the thought of free education

> *'an outrageous slur on the conduct of parents [suggesting] they [are] unconscious of their natural obligations'*[80].

With attitudes such as this, it is hardly surprising that completely free schooling was not introduced until 1902, although a grant of up to ten shillings per pupil in 1891 had gone a long way towards this.

In the early decades of state-provided education, not a great deal of attention was paid to issues which today are central to debates on educational policy: matters such as the content and range of what is taught, the methods of teaching and assessment, and the size and quality of the teaching profession[81]. There was no national curriculum, for example. As might be expected, religious teaching was central to what went on in the church schools but for this to stand any chance of being effective pupils would also need to be taught to read. From 1870, reading and writing were also seen as the essentials in board schools. With the addition of arithmetic to form the alliterative if hardly literate "3Rs", the curriculum of some schools extended no further. For a while, elementary schools were discouraged from broadening the curriculum by the 'payment by results' system. This system (since alternatively labelled the *'maximum literacy at minimum cost'* system[82]) preceded the 1870 Act and to some extent determined how much money each school could get from the government to supplement its other income. The annual government grant, and thereby the salaries of the teachers, depended in part on the number of pupils passing annual examinations in the 3Rs – and *only* the 3Rs.

The subject content of education was further limited by a method of teaching common for much of the 19th century. This was the 'monitorial' system, developed by both the Anglican and the Nonconformist branches of the voluntary schools. Cheap to run, but limited in effectiveness, one teacher or 'master' would teach a select group of older pupils (the monitors) who would then, in turn, instruct the other children. The instruction took the form of 'mechanical drilling', in spelling for example, relying heavily on parrot-fashion repetition and rote-learning. Collectively, pupils might be required to chant the alphabet or their 'times tables'[83].

In some parts of the country countervailing pressures were at work, however. Often with the encouragement of individual inspectors, some schools began to experiment with additions to the curriculum. As early as 1871, for example, a new Board School in Leeds was boasting of at least three qualified teachers and that for the older boys it would offer *'higher instruction in ... science and art'* whilst classes in *'needle-work and domestic economy'* would be provided for girls[84]. A generation later, in neighbouring Bradford, a wide-ranging test paper set by the local School Board contained questions not only in the 3Rs but also in Science, Geography, History, French, and *'Euclid and Algebra (Boys only)'*[85]. Admittedly, the examination was for 'candidate monitors' some of whom could be as old as 15 and for whom this might be an early step along the road to becoming teachers themselves. But it nonetheless shows how far the curriculum in some working class schools had expanded by the turn of the century. Even the more assiduous of today's Year 11 school students might find some of the questions challenging. And for those who believe that the school curriculum should become more 'relevant', how about this for an 'elementary science' question requiring an application of theory to everyday life:

> *'Question 4. Explain how you would determine the Latent Heat of Steam. How does a knowledge of this subject become useful in Cookery?'*

On the other hand, the Geography question which asks: *'How would you prove that the British Isles occupy the best geographical position in the world?'* merely reflects the arrogance of a nation besotted by Empire and is just plain silly. It does suggest, however, how the predominance of the scriptures and religion was giving way to other influences in shaping school curricula by the early 1900s[86]. The business concerns often expressed around the times of the 1870 Act were widening. Industrialists in some districts were finding it hard to recruit appropriately educated workers as technicians. Businesses found they needed school leavers with more than a basic education to fill the expanding number of office jobs that were resulting from firms becoming larger.

In addition to a widening curriculum, in some parts of the country – London was the prime example – school boards had also proved successful in significantly raising educational standards by improving the quality of teaching and providing better school buildings and equipment. The picture in many rural areas was very different, however, with inactive or inefficient school boards or where the boards were under the effective control of supporters of the voluntary organisations whose primary interests were not always those of the state school pupils. Even by the 1890s, the quality and scope of education in some rural schools had not changed greatly from what it had been much earlier in the century[87]. In 1902, the government decided to get rid of the boards and to place the responsibility for elementary education with the county and county borough councils.

In the 32 years that the school boards existed, therefore – from the

1870 Education Act to their abolition – their record of achievement was patchy. Some major developments within elementary education had occurred. Schooling was now available to virtually all children and was free. School attendance was compulsory, the school leaving age had been raised and the curriculum in many schools broadened. Yet none of these things had dented the strongly divided, and divisive, nature of Britain's social structure. Few of the underlying, or even openly expressed, reasons for the development of a national system of elementary schooling had much to do with the interests of the working classes themselves. Although the 1870 Act had laid the foundations which would make schooling for all a reality, it would still very much be education according to social class. The children of the middle classes continued to be educated in a variety of private schools and local grammar schools, and the upper classes still sent their offspring to the large 'public' schools such as Eton, Harrow and Winchester[88]. The novelist and social commentator H G Wells wrote that the 1870 Education Act

> '...was not an Act for common universal education, it was an Act to educate the lower classes for employment on lower class lines, and with specially trained, inferior teachers...'[89]

Similarly, the motives for schooling the working classes had little to do with notions of opportunities for achievement or the realisation of academic potential. Even less were they about avenues of social mobility[90]. Such lofty ideals were not to feature as realistic expectations until well into the 20th century. In fact, as the old Queen drew her last breath, neither elementary education nor the railways looked set to be the social levellers or harbingers of class death that some had hoped for and others had feared.

As the Sproston family would experience a little later in the new century, however, education did play a part in the movement of people away from the village. But it was the railways that more obviously delivered not only geographical mobility but much else besides. The railways have been described as *'Britain's greatest contribution to the modern world'*[91]. Since then, the building of a railway network has normally been considered the essential first part of the infrastructure needed for a country to industrialise. It was certainly fundamental to developing the economies of the two super-powers of the 20th century: the USA and the USSR[92]. And it was the super-power of the 19th century that had supplied engineering skills, labour, capital and, in some cases, hardware that had been responsible for much of the initial railway development overseas.

Christian Wolmar summarises the impact of the railways by emphasising how they:

> '...transformed Britain. They made possible journeys that a generation before would have seemed completely implausible. They boosted all kinds of trade, stimulated economic development, brought in their wake a whole host of social and political changes, and played a vital part when the country went to war.'[93]

When it came, the decline of the British railway industry, most notable in the inter-war years of the 20th century, was not caused by competition from road transport alone. The policies of successive governments often did not help, for example. But it was the rise of the motor car, the motor bus and the motor lorry which signalled clearly some of the relative disadvantages of transport on fixed tracks.

Locally, the two railway lines through the village are still busy today – with the Trent Valley line still forming part of the principal route for travellers between London and Liverpool, Manchester and Glasgow[94]. But the trains no longer stop at the villages – the stations at Colwich and Great Haywood were both closed in the 1950s. No more can villagers travel to work directly by rail, and the days when the railway was a major employer of village labour have long gone.

But in the years between Queen Victoria's death and the end of the Great War, bigger – not always better – things were in store for Nel and some of her brothers. They would show that the railway could not only bring benefits, it could also take away. As Albert Edward prepared to succeed his mother to the throne and to become Edward VII, King of Great Britain and Ireland, Emperor of India and (added for good measure) King of the British Dominions

Beyond the Seas[95], two of the offspring of Little Haywood's Ellen and Christopher Sproston were still to be born. The five already in existence were still children, and four of them were in school. On the eve of the First World War, three had already officially entered adulthood and two were in their teens. The Edwardian era was a period of growing and growing up for Nel and her siblings. The future seemed open, or relatively so, and change was in the air.

Chapter 8

Leaving the Village: (Almost) All Change

The war changed everything. That was how it must have seemed at the time. Nothing would seem the same – and indeed much did change. One historian sums up the impact of the First World War as:

> *'If not exactly a watershed, [then] certainly a steep and sharp waterfall in the course of British history. All the economic, social, cultural, and political forces which... moulded twentieth century Britain were already in flow before 1914, but the war accelerated them with such suddenness and turbulence that they were transformed on a gigantic scale.'*[1]

At a national level, certain economic and political continuities with the pre-war years would emerge as the country started to return to normal. But it was the fractures to family and local life which were most keenly felt and they were more difficult to heal. As the war memorials in virtually every town and village testify, very few places came through the First World War without losing some of their young and not-so-young men. Few families remained untouched by death or disability.

The sheer scale of the devastation to human life left, in the words of Arthur Marwick, *'bitterness and cynicism in its train'*[2]. To this may be added a sense of bewilderment: a not-knowing of why it all happened or what it was all for – and, in the case of relatives at home, a lack of certainty about just what had taken place. Within the space of just two weeks, three of Nel's brothers would leave their Little Haywood home to fight. Two would eventually return but only one would stay. Both had changed. At Ivy Cottage, Nel's maternal grandparents would see out their final days before the war ended. Nel herself would also soon be gone from the village.

But in the years immediately preceding the First World War, life at times would have appeared sunnier. Politicians may have worried about growing unrest among workers, the increasingly militant activities of the suffragettes and the mounting problems in Ireland. But on the other hand, the Boer War had ended in 1902, attitudes to poverty and its causes were starting to change and the government had brought in a series of social reforms that seemed to anticipate the eventual introduction of Britain's Welfare State.

Although perhaps not permanently bathed in the golden glow of the television adaptation of *Lark Rise to Candleford*[3], many aspects of village life in Edwardian Britain continued much as they had done for generations. Even those communities that had been affected more directly by the new systems of communications of the industrial revolution survived by assimilating and working with and around the changes.

Edwardian life at Ivy Cottage would get quite busy at times. In 1911, Christopher, Ellen, all of their seven children (four of them by then teenagers) plus a 22-year old male lodger were living there. There was also the hen. A few chickens would often be kept by villagers, primarily for their eggs, and Ellen would normally have a favourite that would be free to wander – and to lay – indoors[4]. The hallway was quite spacious for a cottage but the rooms less so and the cellar, of course, was where the pig would hang. The facilities were minimal. By the time the cottage was sold following Ellen's death in the 1950s, it still did not have the luxury of an indoor lavatory. And the invention of the flush toilet might just as well never have happened since the outside privy was an earth closet. Over the hole in the ground was strung a wooden bench with two sitting positions. Conditions may have been rudimentary and harsh but at least they could be shared. Night soil men emptied the closet fortnightly[5], when the fragrances from the cottage garden truly came into their own. Although running water was first piped into the village in 1928[6], Nel's father never took advantage of this major boost to domestic convenience. Even in his advancing years, Christopher continued to preserve his complexion by washing in rainwater in the back garden. A large tank against the rear of the house collected surface water from the cottage roof and fed an adjacent stone sink[7]. For a man who eschewed toothpaste, preferring to clean his teeth with a soot-and-salt mixture, this was probably not much of a hardship.

Ivy Cottage became a little less crowded in 1915 as four of the men left home to enlist. But before long domestic adjustments became necessary when Ellen's ailing parents, John and Mary Morris, moved in. Ellen nursed them both until her mother died in October 1917 and her father the following year. Both were buried in Colwich churchyard but in unmarked graves, continuing the sharp social contrasts of village life beyond the lives of its individuals. As would later be the case with their daughter and son-in-law, there was no headstone for the Morrises. By contrast, the final resting places for members of the Anson family of Shugborough are not only elaborately marked but, lying within the church itself, are safely away from the remains of the hoi polloi. One of the latest additions to the private family vaults at Colwich, and secreted behind the choir stalls, is the 5th Earl, the photographer Patrick Lichfield who died in 2005[8].

Not recognised after death maybe, but their dates of birth (both born in 1840) did mark out Ellen's parents for a little good fortune in their later years. They most likely were two of the early beneficiaries of Britain's first state pensions for the elderly. Starting in 1909, pension payments of five shillings per week (25p) were paid to the over 70s provided their income from any other source did not exceed £21 a year. Mary and John would have qualified on age in 1910. Once they had moved into Ivy Cottage, Ellen's parents would only need to cross the road to collect their weekly pension from the Post Office. By this time, their nephew Albert was no longer running the show there. But, in any case, it is unlikely that the new postmistress was still being greeted with the same effusion as that described by writer Flora Thompson in her memories of the Oxfordshire village of her childhood:

'When … the Old Age Pensions began, life was transformed for … aged cottagers. They were relieved of anxiety. They were suddenly rich. Independent for life! At first when they went down to the Post Office to draw it, tears of gratitude would run down the cheeks of some, and they would say as they picked up their money, …"God

bless you, miss" and there were flowers from their gardens and apples from their trees for the girl who merely handed them their money."[9]

The introduction of the old age pension did lessen the risk – but did not completely remove it – of ending one's days in the dreaded workhouse. The measure was modest in its coverage and in the amounts paid out, however, and there were also many exclusions to its entitlement. But it was a start, and the old age pension was just one of a series of social reforms brought in by Liberal governments between 1906 and 1911. Taken together with provisions for cheap school meals, obligatory medical inspections in elementary schools, the introduction of labour exchanges and the start of a national

Nel's maternal grandparents John and Mary Morris: two of the early beneficiaries of the first state pensions

insurance scheme, it seemed to some that the laissez-faire tide of the Victorian era was beginning to turn.

Family life at Ivy Cottage was probably little different from many others in the village. The size of the family is large by today's standards but not unusual in Edwardian England. Christopher is remembered as a kindly man but his reluctance to adopt the practices and accept the comforts of the 20th century, at home or at work, suggests his values were firmly set in the Victorian era. Responsibility for the day-to-day upbringing of children would rest with the mother, assisted by any older daughters. Ellen's attitude to children could be ambivalent. Living into her nineties, she accumulated not only grandchildren but a growing collection of great-grandchildren, too. A framed photograph of each great-grandchild was displayed on the crowded mantelpiece and to each of these children she left a Victorian crown (five shilling) piece. But images and memories are one thing, the activities of real children another – more noisy and less predictable. One granddaughter recalls Ellen's increasing irritation when the especially tempting Ivy Cottage banister rails were repeatedly used as a slide. 'Oh, do stop that, dear', was the standard admonishment[10]. There was a family whisper that Ellen preferred sons and even that one of her daughters was sent away to spend part of her childhood with relatives in Cheshire. This has not been confirmed, however, and if it ever did occur the daughter concerned – Nel – never spoke of it.

It was the Great War that finally ended the days of sunshine and gentle progress of the Edwardian years. The links back to industrialisation are clearly traceable. Conflicts arose as European nations continued their policies of colonisation. The economic explosions generated by the industrial revolution greatly contributed to the competitive scramble for new colonies to provide fresh sources of raw materials and markets for manufactured goods. The ways in which the war was fought – the technology of war – was also significantly determined by the developments of that period. And, once again, a significant role would be played by the railways.

During the First World War, and for three years after, the railways in effect operated under government control[11]. The railways had assisted in the movement of troops in previous conflicts, even as far back as the Crimean War in the 1850s. But without the central role of rail transport, the sheer scale of mobilisation of people, equipment and provisions that took place between 1914 and 1918 would not have been possible[12]. It would start when men first enlisted. In total, about five million men left their towns and villages to serve in the First World War. Many would die, often a long way from home, and it is doubtful that many of those who did return would do so unchanged by their experiences. Some towns and villages suffered a disproportionate loss of their young men. In Middlewich, the ancestral home of the Sprostons, ten percent of the male population aged 15-45 died[13]. A memorial lych-gate at Colwich Church lists the local men who did not return, including one of the sons of Christopher and Ellen. Volunteers from the Haywoods and Colwich travelled by train to join their regiments. All four of the Sproston brothers old enough, or claiming to be old enough, volunteered. Over a two-week period in late February/early March, 1915, Nel watched three of them – including twin Jack – leave Ivy Cottage to start their military training.

Army recruits at Colwich Station, about 1915. The recruits awaiting departure are accompanied by a police officer and a local councillor [Courtesy of Staffordshire Archives and Heritage]

Hazel joined the Royal Engineers. He would later tell his family that his name had at first triggered some stick from his fellow soldiers[14]. Soon, though, they would all have far more serious matters to contend with. Hazel first saw active service in Egypt in 1915 but may have also served, and been wounded, at Gallipoli[15]. He was demobilised in March 1919 but as a Class Z Reserve, which meant that as a trained soldier he could be recalled quickly should hostilities resume[16]. In the event, this was not required and Hazel settled back into his printing career. After leaving school, he had embarked on a long apprenticeship as a News Compositor[17], working at the *Staffordshire Advertiser*. He married in 1921, had one daughter and lived in the nearby village of Milford. Hazel died in 1969, aged 78.

In the decades after the war, Nel probably saw less of her eldest brother than she did of her other siblings and referred to him least in family conversations. As a result of his wartime experiences, and after his marriage, Hazel may have withdrawn more into the private life of his own family. There was also an episode in the 1950s which led to a rift between Hazel on the one side and Nel and her sister on the other. Although the estrangement lessened over time, the distance between them probably never completely closed.

Albert was the youngest of the Sprostons to volunteer. He enlisted with the North Staffordshires (an Infantry regiment) at the age, it appears, of just 16. This was below the minimum age for recruitment, but not always were many questions asked. He was also probably quite tall for his age and would have passed for older. As is the case with his two soldier brothers, Albert's official service records were among those destroyed as a result of enemy bombing in the Second World War. But, for Albert, very little alternative written evidence exists. According to family narrative, however, he experienced warfare on the Western Front where he was wounded. In 1957, admitted to hospital not long before he died, an exploratory surgical operation revealed a bullet still lodged in his body[18].

The cause of Albert's death, in his fifties, however, was more directly related to his fondness for alcohol. It is said that his heavy drinking started as a young man when the woman to whom he was due to marry broke off their engagement[19]. But problems with alcohol are probably often multi-causal: we do not know, for example, if Albert's exposure as a teenager to the horrors of the trenches can at least partially account for how he handled subsequent difficulties and disappointments in his life. A niece who knew Albert well describes him as tall and handsome. She reports that over the years he had a number of girlfriends but that his excessive drinking was responsible for each relationship eventually floundering. After the war, Albert spent the rest of his life in the village. For over twenty years, he helped his father with work on the smallholding and with the milk and coal deliveries. By the early 1940s, however, the family business was waning. Christopher had always been reluctant to chase up customers who were slow to pay for their milk or coal (it was often the better-off customers who were the worst offenders)[20]. But he was now in his late 70s and deserved to be slowing down in any case. So Albert secured a job on the railways as a platelayer, but continued to live with his parents at Ivy Cottage[21].

The tentacles of war stretch long into the future. Nel never quite got over what happened to Jack. Separated from her twin at the age of 22, she never even knew much of what happened to him. She knew that No. 740966 Private John Colin Sproston died on 20 October 1918 in India, aged 25. She also knew that he had died following an illness and not from injuries sustained in battle. But she was probably never told of other details contained in the letter from Jack's Commanding Officer which was sent to her father. And it is doubtful that any member of her family was ever aware of the obituary that appeared in the regimental magazine early the following year. Jack died from pneumonia, a result of the influenza he contracted when the 'Spanish Flu' pandemic had reached that part of India where he was stationed. Between 50 and 100 million people were killed worldwide by this devastating airborne virus. Although it was common for people to make a quick recovery, young adults were particularly prone to the worst effects of the disease:

'Onset was devastatingly quick. Those fine and healthy at breakfast could be dead by tea-time. Within hours of feeling the first symptoms of fatigue, fever and headache, some victims would rapidly develop *pneumonia and start turning blue, signalling a shortage of oxygen. They would then struggle for air until they suffocated to death.'*[22]

The end of Jack's life would quite likely have been a lonely one and it occurred in what to someone brought up amidst the green fields of England must have seemed a harsh, unforgiving place. Temporarily, he was working away from his regiment. He had volunteered or was ordered (in military contexts the distinction is not always clear) to return to the small city of Tank on the North-West Frontier to take charge of water supply and sanitation arrangements, probably in preparation for the further military developments which took place in the region some months later. At the time, his fellow soldiers were based 500 miles to the south-east in the far more equable climate of the foothills of the Himalayas[23].

Like his older brother, Hazel, Jack had worked in the printing industry after leaving school, as a 'jobbing machinist'[24]. For at least part of the time he was at the same newspaper as Hazel. By all accounts, he was an athletic young man, interested in most sports and, once he had made the decision to enlist in the army, these interests accounted for his seemingly unusual choice of regiment. On 9 March 1915 he travelled to Putney Bridge where he joined the 25th Battalion of the London Regiment[25]. This was a Cyclist Battalion, since described as *'the most noted cycle unit in the world'*[26]. The writer of Jack's obituary was to record: *'He was not a native of London, but came up from Staffordshire in order to enlist in a cyclist corps'*[27]. Jack proved to be popular with his fellow soldiers and was known and liked throughout the battalion. The fact that he played football not only for his platoon and company but also for the battalion no doubt helped[28].

At the beginning of the War there were 14,000 cyclists, in various regiments and battalions, in the British Army. At the end this had increased to 100,000. The battalion that Jack joined was used in the early stages to patrol sections of the south and east coast on the lookout for invasions of German troops. Once attacks by air had begun – the first Zeppelin raids were in early 1915 – tasks included cycling the area warning people to take cover and helping to deal with any resultant fires[29]. In February 1916, soldiers of Jack's battalion were shipped to India. Departing from Devonport, they sailed on HMT Ceramic to Bombay and thence to Bangalore in southern India. Jack would never again set foot in England.

From May to December of 1917, Jack and the other soldiers in his company had been involved in the Waziristan Campaign. Waziristan is a mountainous region in what is now North-West Pakistan, bordering Afghanistan. It has long been regarded as one of the world's most dangerous regions and, according to US president Obama, it is *the* most dangerous place. It is home to the two main Pashtun tribes – the Wazir and the Meshud – and the Pakistan Taliban is based there. The violence, including the American policy of concentrating its drone strikes in the tribal areas of the border region, has resulted in the displacement of about half of the population, including 200,000 Meshud[30].

British governments have viewed the region as problematic since the days of Empire when the first attempts at imposing any form of central control over the tribal areas were made[31]. Until partition in 1947, the areas were part of undivided British India. Indian troops defended the border, the North-West Frontier, against encroachments from Afghanistan – the routes through the Khyber and Bolan passes being especially vulnerable. Afghan neutrality was officially maintained during the First World War and many Indian troops were called upon to fight elsewhere. In their place, some troops from Britain – including Jack's battalion – were brought in to defend the area from local attacks. Skirmishes with the Meshud tribe had escalated during 1917 and the Waziristan Campaign was the attempt to deal with the situation militarily. From the descriptions of soldiers involved in the campaign, it seems they were still expected to implement the 'butcher and bolt' policy long employed by the British government through its troops along the Afghan border. Similar to the American strategy during the Vietnam War half a century later, this involved the ransacking and burning of tribal villages, the slaughter of the inhabitants and the destruction of their crops[32].

On the face of it, it appears odd – perverse even – that a battalion of cyclists should be sent to some of the world's most mountainous regions. Bicycles would not seem to be the transport of choice for the rugged terrain and heights of the Afghan border or even for the slopes of the Himalayan foothills. The bicycles of the 25th, however, did not accompany the troops to India. They were left back in England and the soldiers became infantrymen. This was not uncommon during the First World War; cycle battalions were quite often in practice disbanded. There is some irony in the fact that in 1916 – the same year that the men of the 25th were shipped, minus their cycles, to India – Indian troops were transported to France and provided with ... bicycles[33].

During the Campaign, Jack's company was based at Tank – at the edge of the Waziristan region, north-west of the Indus river. Jack's times at Tank and through the Waziristan Campaign would have been miserable. The diaries and memoirs of some of the soldiers paint a picture of relentless and intense heat, lack of water, disease, sandfly fever, mosquito bites and the ever-present threat of malaria, heat stroke, persistent diarrhoea, dust storms, long marches over brutally stony ground, and the danger of being picked off by a random bullet from the surrounding hills and mountains[34]. Neither the city nor the region lent itself to pleasant memories:

'Tank will be remembered for...most of the unpleasant things in life and death except chilblains and fog.'[35]

But even the second exception is disputed by the diary entry of Private Parker:

'Tank is not a very attractive place... It is a flat, dusty country dotted about with palm trees and the heat is terrible... The worst experience we had there, in my opinion, was the dust storms. When these came on it turned day into night and looked like a thick London fog. It was a struggle to breathe, and impossible to see. After one of these it was impossible to get oneself or one's kit clean again for days.'[36]

At the conclusion of the Waziristan campaign, the battalion returned to Jullundur in Punjab, moving on to Jutogh, Shimla during Easter 1918[37]. At the time, and as Simla, this was the summer capital of the British in India and is now a desirable holiday destination famed for its climate, Victorian architecture and spectacular Himalayan views. Jack's time there would have provided a welcome respite before his fateful move back to Tank later in the year. His death there occurred just three weeks before the end of the First World War, although it would be a further twelve months before survivors of the battalion returned home and the battalion disbanded. In the meantime, a detachment from the 25th was sent to help quell an uprising in the city of Amritsar in April 1919. With the exception of a sergeant acting as bodyguard to the officer in charge, however, this contingent was not involved in the massacre which followed. In *'one of the most ignominious episodes in the history of British imperial rule'*, Brigadier-General Reginald Dyer ordered the slaughter by machine-gun fire of hundreds of unarmed people gathered at a public meeting[38].

If there can ever be a place where Jack would have been happy to be laid to rest, it is doubtful that Tank would be it. But buried there he was – in Tank Cemetery 36[39]. Twin sister Nel never knew where or even if he was buried. Neither did she know that Jack was commemorated on India Gate in Delhi, a massive stone arch standing 40 metres high and spanning 15 metres. The memorial lists the names of 13,300 soldiers but commemorates all 70,000 *soldiers of undivided India who fell in defence of the British Empire 1914-1921'* plus those from UK and Australian forces. Over a thousand of those listed by name, including Jack, were buried in cemeteries to the west of the River Indus *'where maintenance was not possible'*[40]. Closer to home, a general memorial to members of the 25th battalion who died during the Great War can be found on the west end wall of All Saints Church at Putney Bridge. Nel died unaware of its existence.

More than a year after Jack died, his father received a sum of money from the War Office for the back-pay owed to Jack. The amount was £54-4s-6d (£54.23).

Of Nel's remaining brothers and sisters, Bill, the middle child, also had some military involvement during the war, serving as a private in the Northumberland Fusiliers and the York and Lancaster regiments[41]. Bill, short for William, would have been conceived shortly before his grandfather's fatal accident and was named after him. After leaving school, his first job had been as a farm labourer

Private J Sproston, died at Tank 20 October 1918

on his father's smallholding. He married a local girl in 1919 and they had two children. Although they eventually moved away permanently from Little Haywood, they did not go far. The family took on a farm near to the village of Colton, a few miles from the Haywoods, where Bill and his wife continued to live and work until Bill's death in 1965 at the age of 69.

Unlike her brothers and sisters, Rene never lived anywhere except the village. Even Albert spent some time away during the First World War. Rene was married, at the age of 25, to a local railway employee who worked as a porter at Colwich Station. She lived to the age of 92.

Bernard was the youngest. Hazel, the eldest, was already 13 years old when his fourth brother was born. A quiet, nervous and introverted child, Bernard would sometimes be teased by his brothers and sisters for his lone interests which could absorb him for long periods. Bernard and a visiting owl could spend motionless hours staring at each other in the back garden. Mother Ellen eventually put a stop to this budding engagement with wildlife when her young son's owl-blinking emulations started to intrude into his human interactions[42].

Bernard grew up to be tall and slim, slow in speech and

unhurried in movement. The anxieties of childhood produced an anxious adult. Sensitive to the needs of others, even to the point of over-empathising, he was caring and was always popular with children in the family. Adults would occasionally become impatient with his hesitant and circuitous way of talking, particularly over the telephone. But they were very fond of him, too, so 'Get to the point, Bernard' was generally thought rather than said. He married at the age of 23 and went on to have three children. The family lived in the nearby town of Rugeley. Bernard died in 1993, in his 89th year.

Eventually, then, Christopher and Ellen would see all their children leave the village with the exception of Rene. Once he had returned from the war, Albert, too, would become a permanent resident of Little Haywood, spending the last few years of his life with his younger sister's family. But the remaining four Sproston children – Hazel, Nel, Bill and Bernard – would make their homes elsewhere.

In their own ways, both the railways and elementary schooling provided an escape route from the village. Although social mobility had most definitely not been the intention behind the universal provision of elementary education, one consequence of mass schooling was that it did enable a degree of geographical mobility. With the ability to read and write, children of the later Victorian and Edwardian eras could train in jobs that did not require young adults to stay in the village where their parents grew up. This was just as well since the steep decline in the numbers employed in agriculture continued after the First World War[43]. With fewer job prospects within the village, teenagers and young adults moved into or closer to the towns of Stafford, Rugeley and Lichfield or even farther afield. And during and after the First World War it was the railways that often facilitated the geographical movements, even those over relatively short distances. With rail links between and rail stations or halts at most towns and villages, people could maintain regular contact with their families of origin even if they were no longer living in the same village. It was in this way that Little Haywood remained the hub of the increasingly dispersed Sproston clan.

Nel, for example, would make frequent visits back to the village of her birth and to the parental home right up until the death of her mother Ellen at the age of 91 in 1953. This occasion closed the half-century Sproston connection with Ivy cottage. Events following produced a split within the family that was not healed for many years. Hazel had bought the cottage for his parents while they were both still alive, but retained legal ownership. After his mother died he decided to sell the property. The problem, however, was that Albert was still living there. Hazel evicted his younger brother who found himself homeless. He was taken in by sister Rene and her family who lived in a small two-bedroom cottage just down the road. To make space for their new lodger, the bedroom of Rene and her husband had now to accommodate their 20-year old daughter, too. To add insult to injury, Ivy Cottage was sold to a neighbour with whom Ellen had long been in dispute over a shared driveway. As a result of Hazel's actions, Rene and Nel refused to have anything to do with their eldest brother for a long time[44].

Christopher and Ellen in the garden of Ivy Cottage

As there was no rail stop at Little Haywood, visitors to Ivy Cottage would alight at Colwich Station, if travelling on the Trent Valley line, or at Great Haywood on the Knotty. Either way, there would then be a walk of under a mile. Although little separates the three linear villages in distance, each arguably retains a distinct personality. Can a certain aloofness still be detected in Great Haywood, for example – a reminder of its historical connections with its posh neighbour, Shugborough? Does it see itself today as the place that attracts the tourists through its strategic location for canal boat holidays? Perhaps Colwich's local presence is imbued with a whiff of superiority, lending its name to the wider parish council and housing the ancient church with its tombs stuffed with dead aristocrats. Godless Little Haywood, in comparison, has been the slightly rebellious child keen to exert its independence – but only up to a point.

Even if not entirely fanciful, these differences should not be exaggerated, however. The broad historical trajectories of the villages have important antecedents in common. The original settlements owe much to the line of the river where the Trent Valley narrows as it edges the higher ground of Cannock Chase[45]. For centuries this corridor provided the locals with good grazing land for their cattle and sheep. Over the past two-and-a-half centuries, the physical, economic and social contours of Little Haywood, and those of its neighbouring villages to each side, have been redrawn as a direct result of the industrial revolution. A fundamental part of Britain's industrialisation consisted of successive developments in transport and systems of communications. The building of the canals and innovations in road construction and travel were essential to getting the whole process off the ground. The coming of the railways ensured that the momentum was maintained.

Little Haywood is by no means unique in being directly affected by these developments, but the developments are displayed there particularly graphically. The near-parallel paths of river, canal, roads and railway lines are constant and vivid reminders of their topographical impact. They have helped to shape the lives of generations of its people and perhaps none more so than the Sprostons. It was the canal that first delivered the Sprostons to

Staffordshire as Thomas's narrow boat brought his family over the border from Cheshire. The canal was also responsible for son William's move to Little Haywood and for making the Navigation Inn his family home. Thirty-five years later it was the main London to Chester road that ended William's life. During and soon after the First World War, it was the railway that removed his grandchildren from the village.

One way or another, therefore, the revolutions in transport that were crucial for industrialisation and so important to the modern history of Britain and the world also explain the Sproston move to the village and the departures from it. The canals brought the Sprostons to Little Haywood; the roads and railways took them away.

It was during the Great War that Nel's turn to leave would arrive. She was about to embark on the next stage of her life – independent from Ivy Cottage, her parents and Little Haywood. It would be a long life and one that that would encompass, as most lives do, a mixture of tragedy and success, happiness and sorrow. Nel would know domestic service; she would be happily married but would be widowed relatively early. She would have two children, four grandchildren and five great-grandchildren before her death. She would live through two world wars. She would see the aeroplane become a common form of transport, but would not experience it herself. She did not drive but would regularly be driven in motor cars and she would ride on motor buses. She would live through the heyday of the train and would witness the decline of the canal and the end of the horse-drawn road traffic that had killed her grandfather. Unlike Grandfather William, whom she knew well but did not remember, Jack was never forgotten. Her twin's journey had ended prematurely and so far away. Nel loved him dearly. She would speak of him often and with an almost palpable sense of loss, a sense of loss that never entirely left her.

But just as she never discovered what happened to Jack's body Nel was never told that her grandfather's fatal accident occurred if not on the doorstep of Ivy Cottage then just outside the gate. Sometimes we know just as little about the things that are closest to us as we do of events and developments half a world away. The house where Nel had spent part of her childhood, her teens and her early twenties directly overlooked that fateful pile of stone chippings. She remained unaware of the swerve, the escalating sound of advancing hooves, the sickening crunch of the collision. And she never knew about the broken vehicles, spilled cargo and splintered bodies – human and equine – that littered that part of Little Haywood's Main Road one winter's day in 1896.

For now, though, Nel was packing her bags as she prepared to leave Ivy Cottage and begin her own journey…

Main Road, Little Haywood

View of the centre of Little Haywood from the crossroads. The three-storey building on the left housed the Post Office. The photograph was taken about the time of the family move to Ivy Cottage which is the smaller building at the end of the row of terraced houses to the right of the picture. The next building along, in the centre of the picture, is the Red Lion. This is the stretch of road where William's fatal accident occurred in 1896. [Courtesy of Staffordshire Archives and Heritage]

Source Notes

Foreword

1. The Observer, Sunday 9 July, 2006.

Chapter 1

1. Staffordshire Advertiser, Saturday 21 March 1896, p.5. I am indebted to Colin Sproston for unearthing this report of the inquest into William's death together with other details of his life. Colin is William's great-great-grandson.
2. http://news.bbc.co.uk/2/hi/uk_news/5256506.stm.
3. www.uk-roadsafety.co.uk. (Accessed 2 January 2013)
4. www.familytreetalk.co.uk/bmd.html (Accessed 3 May 2012)
5. Marriage certificate 1 February 1845.
6. Reay 1991.
7. Breach & Hartwell 1972, pp. 25, 34.
8. Bryson 2009, p.33.
9. Staffordshire Advertiser, Saturday 21 March 1896, p.5.
10. Anna Davin, cited in Bryson 2011, p.580.
11. Evans 2010.
12. Hobsbawn 1999, p.50.
13. Lee 1852.
14. Rightmove 2012.
15. Death certificates for John, Ruth, Emma and Alfred Sproston.
16. Atkins 1999.
17. 'Final Report from Her Majesty's Commissioners on Agriculture, 1882, C. 3309, vol.XIV.
18. Mathias 2001, pp.312-319.
19. Court 1967, p.195.
20. Mathias 2001, pp.361-9.
21. May 1996, p.123.
22. Ashworth 1972, p.46.
23. May 1996, p.126.

24. Saul, 1969, p.55.

25. Mathias 2001, pp.361-9.

26. Bryson 2011, pp.621-2.

27. University of Portsmouth 2009 (www.visionofbritain.org.uk/ – census data for parish of Colwich) (Accessed 30 April 2012)

28. Ashworth 1972, pp.63-4.

29. The Cornhill Magazine, Vol. 29 (1874), pp.686-697; included as Agricultural Labourers (1874), www.victorianweb.org/history/work/html (Accessed 18 June 2012)

30. May 1996, p.107.

31. Mr G Alston of St Philip's, Bethnal Green quoted in Engels 1969, p.62-3.

32. From an article in the October, 1843 issue of The Artisan on the sanitary condition of working people in cities; quoted in Engels 1969, p.71.

33. Engels 1969, pp. 82-3.

34. Marx 1976, p.817.

35. Eighth Public Health Report of the Medical Officer of the Privy Council, 1866 (quoted in Marx 1976, pp. 817-8).

36. Mingay 1990, pp.86-7.

Chapter 2

1. Lawrence H Officer & Samuel H Williamson, 'Purchasing Power of British Pounds from 1245 to Present', MeasuringWorth, 2011. URL: www.measuringworth.com/ppoweruk/. The values given are based on comparisons of the years 1896 and 2010. The lower value is based on a purchasing power calculator which uses the RPI (the Retail Price Index); the higher value assesses the wealth in relation to the total output of the economy (the share of Gross Domestic Product).

2. England & Wales, National Probate Calendar (Index of Wills and Administrations), 1858-1966.

3. Death certificate of John Sproston.

4. Death certificate of son Alfred Sproston, July 1877.

5. Pennant 1811, p.107.

6. visionofbritain.org.uk; and Stafford Borough Council, 2012, p.42.

7. Colwich Parish Council undated, p.2.

8. Bradley et al 1997, p.6.

9. Bradley et al 1997, p.8.

10. Bradley et al 1997, pp.8-9, 37-8, 83.

11. Bradley et al 1993, p.5.

12. Lists of services facilities at the two villages can be found at Stafford Borough Council 2012, pp.20, 31-3, 39.

13. Staffordshire Past-Track, 'Wooden Footbridge, Little Haywood', www. search.staffspasttrack.org.uk/engine/resource/default.asp?txtKeywords= Weetman%27s+B... (Accessed 13 August, 2012)

14. Institute for Name-Studies, University of Nottingham. www.Nottingham. ac.uk/key.aspx. (Accessed 13 August 2012)

15. Morris 1976, 2,5. 247a.

16. Staffordia 1930, pp.7, 48.

17. Colwich Parish Council undated, p.7.

18. Tom Fort, 'River Trent: Going with the flow of history', The Telegraph (posted 15th March 2008), www.telegraph.co.uk/earth/3336220/River-Trent-Going-with-the- flow-of-history.htm. (Accessed 26 June 2012)

19. 'Trent history', www.ontrent.org.uk/site/pages/trent-history. (Accessed 26 June 2012).

20. Colwich Parish Council undated, p.2.

21. Robert Mountford, 'Portrait of the Trent', www.saltbox.org.uk. (Accessed 28 June 2012).

22. Colwich Parish Council undated, p.2.

23. UK Battlefields Resource Centre, The Battlefields Trust, www. battlefieldstrust.com/resource-centre/civil-war/battleview.asp?Battle FieldId=19. (Accessed 29 June 2012)

24. Colwich Parish Council undated, p.2.

25. Bradley et al 1993, pp.6-7.

26. www.geograph.org.uk/article/River-Trent---The-Staffordshire-Trent. (Accessed 29 June 2012)

27. Staffordshire Past-Track, www.staffspasttrack.org.uk. This is Staffordshire County Council's valuable online searchable archive of the county's cultural heritage and community history materials.

28. www.transportheritage.com/find-heritage-locations.html?sobi2Task=sobi2 Details&sobi2ld=601. (Accessed 17 July 2012)

29. Merrill 1989, p.35.

30. Fort 2009, p.80.

31. Staffordshire Past-Track, www.staffspasttrack.org.uk.

32. Staffordia 1930, pp.47, 54.

33. Pennant 1811, p.90.

34. Fort 2009, p.79.

35. Sproston 2007, pp.61, 64-5; 'On the Tolkien Trail', http://www.moathouse.co.uk/
    resources/uploads/files... (Accessed 30 July 2013); BBC Staffordhire, 'Tolkien's
    Staffordshire Past', October 2004, http://www.bbc.co.uk/stoke/features/2003/01/
    Tolkien.shtml; http://ianweightman.co.uk/blog/the-hobbit-tolkien-shugborough-
    and-the-forest-... (Accessed 30 July 2013); Bradley et al 1997, p.94.

36. www.rugeleypower.com. (Accessed 30 June 2012)

37. www.geograph.org.uk/article/River-Trent---The-Staffordshire-Trent.
    (Accessed 29 June 2012)

38. Briggs undated, p.3; Brown 2010, p.103.

39. Tom Fort, 'River Trent: Going with the flow of history', The Telegraph
    (posted 15th March 2008), www.telegraph.co.uk/earth/3336220/River-Trent-
    Going-with-the- flow-of-history.htm. (Accessed 26 June 2012)

40. Greenslade & Stuart 1984, p.77.

41. Colwich Parish Council undated, p.2.

42. Fort 2009, p.101.

43. Colwich Parish Council undated, pp.3,4.

44. Bradley et al 1997, p.14.

Chapter 3

1. The Sproston Family History Site (freepages.genealogy.rootsweb.ancestry.
   com/~sprostonfamily) contains a wealth of information on the different
   'branches' of the Sproston line. The term 'yeoman' appears quite frequently
   in historical texts yet its meaning is somewhat ambiguous. It seems to
   indicate a mixture of occupation and status, referring to a class of freeholders,
   ranking somewhere below the gentry, who cultivate the land.

2. Sproston Family History site (see Note 1 above). (Accessed 15 May 2012)

3. O'Riordan 1986.

4. In O'Riordan 1986.

5. O'Riordan 1986.

6. O'Riordan 1986.

7. www.gbnames.publicprofiler.org (Accessed 15 May 2012)

8. The Sproston Pages: freepages.genealogy.rootsweb.ancestry.com/~sproston/
   origins.html. (Accessed 15 May 2012). See also Name Origin Research:
   www.surnamedb.com 1980-2012 (Accessed 4 June 2012)

9. Sproston Parish Council website: www.sprostonparishcouncil.org.uk (Accessed: 15 May 2012)

10. Hobsbawm 1962.

11. For a contemporary analysis of the events in France of 1848 and beyond, see Marx, 1964. A briefer description and interpretation of the 'June days' insurrection in Paris and its brutal suppression can be found in Marx's 'The Eighteenth Brumaire of Louis Bonaparte' (in Marx & Engels 1968, pp.94-179), particularly in Section 1. For a more recent and entertaining account of the events of 1789 and after, see Steel 2004.

12. Greenslade & Stuart 1984, p.87.

13. Thompson 1967, p.60.

14. Roberts 1982, particularly pp.56-61.

15. Townsend 1979. For attempts to measure poverty over time, see for example Haughton & Khandker 2009, Chapter 11.

16. On the standard of living debate, see, for example, Thompson 1968 and Hobsbawm 1968.

17. University of Portsmouth (www.visionofbritain.org.uk – population data for London and Manchester) (Accessed 19 September 2012)

18. Engels 1969, p.37.

19. May 1996, p.3.

20. Greenslade & Stuart 1984, p.86.

21. Welch 1997.

22. Greenslade & Stuart 1984, pp.85,86.

23. Greenslade & Stuart 1984, p.86.

24. www.middle-ages.org.uk/feudalism.htm. (Accessed 10 September 2012)

25. Dobb 1963, p.6.

26. www.middle-ages.org.uk/feudalism.htm. (Accessed 10 September 2012)

27. Engels 1957; Dobb 1963, p.11.

28. Perkin 1970, p.36.

29. Court 1967, p.43.

30. Mathias 2001, pp.115-6.

31. The debate is fundamentally about the development of capitalism, and the reasons for it. The starting points are normally seen as the writings of Karl Marx in the mid-19th century and the work of Max Weber writing a generation or so later. For those brave or foolhardy enough to consult the originals, see Marx 1976, Part 8 and Weber 1930.

32. Reported in Bradley et al 1997, p.97.

33. Perkin 1970, p.43.

34. Bradley et al 1997, p.77.

Chapter 4

1. Kelly's Directory of Staffordshire, 1896, p.123.

2. Kelly's Directory of Staffordshire, 1900, pp.128-9; UK census 1901.

3. Stafford Record Office, Document D615/EL/8/259 'Leases & Agreements: Haywood Park Farm', 1897(part of the 'Records of the Anson Family of Shugborough, Earls of Lichfield' collection).

4. Kelly's Directory of Staffordshire, 1900, pp.128-9.

5. The 1901 census has been the starting point for much of the information in this paragraph.

6. Gascoigne, Bamber, 'History of Canals', HistoryWorld, from 2001, ongoing. http://historyworld.net/wrldhis/PlainTextHistories.asp?historyid=aa19. (Accessed 27 August 2012)

7. Gascoigne (see Note 6 above).

8. Pennine Waterways, 'History of the Bridgewater Canal'. www.penninewaterways.co.uk/bridgewater/bri2.htm. (Accessed 27 August 2012)

9. Gascoigne (see Note 6 above).

10. Norwich Cathedral, 'Founding and Building of the Cathedral'. www.cathedral.org.uk/learning/pupil-papers-founding-and-building-the-cathedral.aspx#top. (Accessed 27 August 2012)

11. Mathias 2001, p.100.

12. Mathias 2001, p.100.

13. Mathias 2001, p.100.

14. Pennine Waterways, 'History of the Sankey Canal'. www.penninewaterways.co.uk/sankey/sa2.htm. (Accessed 27 August 2012)

15. Mathias 2001, p.101.

16. Mathias 2001, p.102.

17. Mathias 2001, pp.97-8.

18. Flinn 1961.

19. Mathias 2001, pp. 98, 107.

20. Mathias 2001, p.52.

21. Allison 1969.

22. Mathias 2001, p.102.

23. Mathias 2001, p.101.

24. Visit Birmingham, 'The history of Birmingham', http://visitbirmingham. com/what-to-do/heritage/the-history-of-birmingham. (Accessed 30 October 2013); and Tim Lambert, 'A brief history of Birmingham, England', http://www.localhistories.org/birmingham.html. (Accessed 30 October 2013)

25. Wilkes 2011, p.75.

26. Wilkes 2011, p.75.

27. Mathias 2001, pp.97-8.

28. Greenslade & Stuart 1984, p.96.

29. British Waterways pamphlet, Trent & Mersey Canal, undated.

30. Staffordshire County Council, Trent and Mersey Canal, Staffordshire County Council Planning & Development Department, 1988. www. eaststaffsbc.gov.uk/Planning/Conservation%20Area%20Appraisals/Tent%20 and%20Mersey%20Canal.pdf. (Accessed 16 October 2012); and Lead 1980, p.46.

31. Staffordshire County Council, Trent and Mersey Canal (see Note 30 above).

32. Greenslade & Stuart 1984, p.96.

33. British Waterways pamphlet, Trent & Mersey Canal, undated.

34. BBC, 'Why the industrial revolution happened here', presented by Jeremy Black, broadcast on BBC2, 14 January 2013.

35. Greenslade & Stuart 1984, p.96.

36. Briggs undated, p.5.

37. Morgan, Tom, 'The sad legacy of Wedgwood', *The Independent*, 5 January, 2009.

38. British Waterways pamphlet, Trent & Mersey Canal, undated.

39. Briggs undated, p.7.

40. www.the-narrowboat.co.uk/Articles/. (Accessed 8 October 2012)

41. Briggs undated, p.7.

42. www.the-narrowboat.co.uk/Articles/.(Accessed 8 October 2012)

43. Briggs undated, p.6.

44. Sandbach Town Council, A Brief History of Sandbach, www.sandbach.gov. uk/brief-history-sandbach.htm (Accessed 9 October 2012)

45. Matthews 2000, p.82.

46. Cheshire Bishops Transcripts 1598-1900.

47. Family trees on www.genesreunited.co.uk.

48. R Clayton Brough, 'The Descendants of Richard Burgh of Windygates, Leek, Staffordshire:1450 to Present', Brough Family Organization, www. broughfamily.org. (Accessed 10 October 2012)

49. *The Cheshire Courant*, Tuesday 19 September, 1809 & Tuesday 17 April 1810; *Chester Chronicle*, Friday 22 September 1809; and the *Manchester Mercury*, Tuesday 8 May 1810.

50. Wilkes 2011, pp.58, 69; Freer 1991, p.228.

51. Freer 1991, p.228.

52. Wilkes 2011, pp.49-50.

53. Wilkes 2011, p.59.

54. Wilkes 2011, p.51.

55. Wilkes 2011, pp.38-9, 41, 45.

56. Freer 1991, pp.128, 280.

57. Cited in Freer 1991, p.222.

58. www.canalcuttings.co.uk/cruisers/trent-and-mersey-part3.html. (Accessed 29 October 2012)

59. Wilkes 2011, pp.37-8.

60. Freer 1991, p.129.

61. Quoted in Wilkes 2011, p.41.

62. Wilkes 2011, p.41; Hanson 1975, p.71; Lindsay 1979, pp.160-161.

63. 'Report Of The Execution Of Christina Collins' Murderers, 1840', William Salt Library: Broadsheets 2/37, www.staffspasttrack.org.uk/exhibit/ArchivesMillennium/1800-1900a.html. (Accessed 21 November 2012)

64. From newspaper report included in 'Report Of The Execution Of Christina Collins' Murderers, 1840', William Salt Library: Broadsheets 2/37, www.staffspasttrack.org.uk/exhibit/ArchivesMillennium/1800-1900a.html. (Accessed 21 November 2012)

65. Wilkes 2011, p.43.

66. Wilkes 2011, p.43.

67. Bradley et al 1997, p.56.

68. Wilkes 2011, p.55.

69. Freer 1991, p.209.

70. Freer 1991, pp.150-2.

71. Freer 1991, pp149-50; 157-8; 243.

72. Wilkes 2011, p.41.

73. Wilkes 2011, pp.42-3.

74. Bradley et al 1997, p.82.

75. Greenslade & Stuart, p.96; Briggs undated, p.5; British Waterways pamphlet, Trent & Mersey Canal, undated; and Wilkes 2011, p.40.

76. Briggs undated, p.6.

77. British Waterways pamphlet, Trent & Mersey Canal, undated.

78. Greenslade & Stuart 1984, p.96.

79. Greenslade & Stuart 1984, p.96.

80. Greenslade & Stuart 1984, p.96.

81. Staffordshire County Council, Trent and Mersey Canal, Staffordshire County Council Planning & Development Department, 1988. www.eaststaffsbc.gov.uk/Planning/Conservation%20Area%20Appraisals/Tent%20and%20Mersey%20Canal.pdf. (Accessed 16 October 2012)

82. Quoted in Staffordshire County Council (see Note 81 above)

83. Carlyle 1977, Book 3: The Modern Worker; Chapter 5: The English.

84. Greenslade & Stuart 1984, p.96.

85. www.canalcruisingguide.com/2012guidept.2pdf. (Accessed 15 October 2012)

86. 'History of Stone', www.into-stone.co.uk/artemps/display6.php3?id=1. (Accessed 3 October 2012) and British Waterways pamphlet, Trent & Mersey Canal, undated.

87. Massey, Donald 'History of Weston', www.westonstaffs.org.uk/details.php?pkid=86 (Accessed 9 July 2012)

88. White 1834, pp.693-4.

89. www.naturalengland.org.uk/ourwork/conservation/geodiversity/englands/counties/area_ID5.aspx. (Accessed 23 October 2012); Colwich Parish Council undated, p.14; www.domesdaybook.net/helpfiles/hs855.htm. (Accessed 24 October 2012); and Bristow 2001, p.197.

90. www.cheshireeast.gov.uk/leisure,_culture_and_tourism/ranger_service/countryside_sites_/congleton_area/rode_heath_rise.aspx. (Accessed 23 October 2012)

91. Cheshire County Council, 'Hassall Green Explorer' leaflet, undated.

92. Twigg, George, D, 'Salt Making Sites in Cheshire', Cheshire Local History Association, www.cheshirehistory.org.uk/salt.html. (Accessed 23 October 2012)

93. British Waterways pamphlet, Trent & Mersey Canal, undated.

94. White 1834, p.694.

95. Katie Martin, 'Hixon's worth its salt', BBC Stoke & Staffordshire, 26 January, 2008, www.bbc.co.uk/print/stoke/content/aticles/2008/01/22/hixon_salt_feature.shtml. (Accessed 5 October 2012)

96. Broadbridge 1970 and White 1834, p.694.

97. Massey, Donald 'History of Weston', www.westonstaffs.org.uk/details.php?pkid=86 (Accessed 9 July 2012)

98. Member family trees on Ancestry.co.uk.

99. Joint Nature Conservation Committee, 'Pasturefields Salt Marsh', www.jncc.defra.gov.uk/protectedsites/sacselection/sac.asp?EUcode=UK0012789. (Accessed 24 October 2012)

100. Morris 1976, 247a (Domesday Book ref: 99 22 2,5).

101. Bradley et al 1997, p.79.

102. 'Tixall Quarries', www.tixall-ingestre-andres.me.uk/tixall/txlqrry.html. (Accessed 24 October 2012)

103. Broadbridge 1970 and 'Tixall Quarries' (see Note 102 above)

104. Broadbridge 1970.

105. Wilkes 2011, p.18.

106. Bradley et al 1997, p.82.

107. Freer 1991, p.40.

108. Freer 1991, p.83.

109. Bradley et al 1997, p.81.

110. Wilkes 2011, p.20.

111. Wilkes 2011, p.101.

112. Colwich Parish Council, undated, p.3.

Chapter 5

1. Department for Transport, 'Road accidents and safety statistics: RAS30', 10 November 2012, www.gov.uk/government/organisations/department-for-transport. (Accessed 2 January 2013)

2. BBC Radio 4, 'More or Less', broadcast 30 December 2012.

3. BBC Radio 4 (see Note 2 above) and 'UK road deaths reach record low', http://news.bbc.co.uk/1/hi/uk/8118341.stm, 25 June 2009. (Accessed 7 January 2013)

4. Bradley et al 1997, p.13.

5. For information on the history of coding/labelling Britain's road system, presented in an entertaining way, see www.cbrd.co.uk/indepth/roadnmbers/history.shtml.

6. Bradley et al 1997, p.56.

7. 1901 census.

8. See, for example, Staffordia 1930, p.18 and British Listed Buildings, Parish Church of St Michael & All Angels, Colwich, http://www.britishlistedbuildings.co.uk/en-443128... (Accessed 29 July 2013)

9. BBC, 'Domesday Reloaded: St Michael's Church, Colwich', 1986, http://

www.bbc.co.uk/history/domesday/dblock/GB-400000-321000/page/4. (Accessed 20 May 2013), and www.staffspasttrack.org.uk.

10. 'Dale-Sproston' family tree on www.ancestry.co.uk.

11. Colwich Parish Council undated, p.2.

12. Greenslade & Stuart 1984, p.91.

13. 'Economic infrastructure and institutions: Roads and transport', A History of the County of Cheshire: Volume 5 part 2: The City of Chester: Culture, Buildings, Institutions, 2005, pp.73-83. URL: www.british-history.ac.uk/report.aspx?compid=57309 (Accessed 19 June 2012)

14. Highways Agency, 'A brief history of our roads', www.highways.gov.uk/knowledge/1813.aspx. (Accessed 19 June 2012)

15. Highways Agency (see Note 14).

16. Old Hampshire Mapped, 'Turnpikes', www.geog.port.ac.uk/webmap/hantsmap/hantsmap/turnpike.htm. (Accessed 10 July 2012)

17. www.worldwidewords.org.qa/qa-tur2.htm. (Accessed 10 July 2012)

18. Albert 2006, and www.geog.port.ac.uk/webmap/hantsmap/hantsmap/turnpike.htm. (Accessed 10 July 2012)

19. Old Hampshire Mapped (see Note 16 above).

20. Highways Agency (see Note 14 above).

21. Flint Local History Society, 'Flint through the ages: turnpike roads and the railway' www.fflint.co.uk/railway.html. (Accessed 15 July 2012), and Highways Agency (see Note 14 above).

22. www.nationalexpress.home.aspx (Accessed 10 July 2012)

23. 'Turnpike roads and the railway', www.fflint.co.uk/railway.html. (Accessed 7 August 2012)

24. 'Turnpike roads and the railway' (see Note 23 above).

25. Mathias 2001, p.97.

26. *Staffordshire Advertiser*, Saturday 21 March, 1896, 'Fatal Trap Accident at Little Haywood', p. 5.

27. www.nationalarchives.gov.uk/education/lesson48.htm. (Accessed 7 January 2013)

28. May 1996, p.46.

29. www.nationalarchives.gov.uk/education/lesson48.htm.

30. www.nationalarchives.gov.uk/education/lesson48.htm.

31. www.nationalarchives.gov.uk/education/lesson48.htm.

32. Mathias 2001, pp.102, 104.

33. Mathias 2001, p.105.

34. http://www.turnpikes.org.uk. (Accessed 17 July 2012)

35. Highways Agency, 'A brief history of our roads', www.highways.gov.uk/knowledge/1813.aspx. (Accessed 19 June 2012)

36. O'Farrell 2008, pp. 276-7.

37. 'Economic infrastructure and institutions: Roads and transport', A History of the County of Cheshire: Volume 5 part 2: The City of Chester: Culture, Buildings, Institutions, 2005, pp.73-83. URL: www.british-history.ac.uk/report.aspx?compid=57309 (Accessed: 19 June 2012)

38. Radio 4 interview, week commencing 19 August 2012.

39. Brown 2010, pp.77-9.

40. Brown 2010, p.65.

41. Brown 2010, pp.73-5.

42. Greenslade 1990, pp.43-47.

43. http://www.turnpikes.org.uk. (Accessed 17 July 2012)

44. 'Economic infrastructure and institutions: Roads and transport', A History of the County of Cheshire: Volume 5 part 2: The City of Chester: Culture, Buildings, Institutions, 2005, pp.73-83. URL: www.british-history.ac.uk/report.aspx?compid=57309 (Accessed: 19 June 2012)

45. Brown 2010, p.75.

46. White 1851, p.358.

47. Flint Local History Society, 'Flint through the ages: turnpike roads and the railway' www.fflint.co.uk/railway.html. (Accessed 15 July 2012), and Highways Agency (see Note 14 above).

48. Pennant 1811.

49. University of Portsmouth, 'Thomas Pennant: The Journey from Chester to London', 2009, www.visionofbritain.org.uk/text/contents_page.jsp?t_id=Pennant_C2L. (Accessed 13 January 2013)

50. BBC, 'Time Traveller's Guide to Elizabethan England', presented by Ian Mortimer, broadcast on BBC2, 9.00pm 7 June 2013.

51. Pennant 1811, p.77.

52. Pennant 1811, p.84.

53. Pennant 1811, pp.84-5.

54. Shirley Family Association, 'Chartley Castle', Shirley Association, undated, http://www.shirleyassociation.com/NewShirleySite/NonMembers/England/chartley.html. (Accessed 13 January 2013)

55. Pennant 1811, p.89.

56. Records of St Andrews Parish Church, Weston – held at Staffordshire Record Office.

57. Massey, Donald 'History of Weston', www.westonstaffs.org.uk/details. php?pkid=86 (Accessed 9 July 2012).

58. Massey, Donald 'History of Weston', www.westonstaffs.org.uk/details. php?pkid=86 (Accessed 9 July 2012).

59. Pennant 1811, p.89.

60. Bradley et al 1993, p.5.

61. Staffordia 1930, p.53.

62. Register of Licensees 1907-1912, Stafford Record Office.

63. '1904 Licensing Act', www.dereham-pubs.co.uk/1904act.html. (Accessed 9 July 2012); Light & Heenan 1999, p.15.

64. Brown 2010, Chap 6.

65. Brown 2010, pp.138-9.

66. Brown 2010, p.138.

67. England & Wales, National Probate Calendar (Index of Wills & Administration), 1861-1941.

68. Bentley et al 1999, p.199.

69. Bentley et al 1999, pp.199-200.

70. Raeburn 1974, pp.260-269.

71. Rowbotham 1973, pp.87-8.

72. Rover 1967; Pugh 1990.

73. Rover 1967.

74. Pugh 1980.

75. Mathias 2001, p.104.

Chapter 6

1. StaffsLive, 18 January 2012, www.staffslive.co.uk/.../residents-say-hs2-will-devastate-small-of-haywood-and-colwich/. (Accessed10 July 2012)

2. Department for Transport, 'HS2 phase two initial preferred route plan and profile maps', 28 January 2013. https://www.gov.uk/hs2-phase-two-initial-preferred-route-plan-and-profile-maps. (Accessed 28 January 2013)

3. Express & Star, 'HS2 will force us out of homes', Express & Star 7 July 2013, http://www.expressandstar.com/news/transport-news/2013/07/07/hs2-will-force-us-out-homes/

4. 'Shugborough', www.staffordshire.gov.uk/leisure/museums/exhibitions/shugborough/Shugborough.aspx (Accessed 14 January 2013); and Kelly's Directory of Staffordshire, 1900, p.128.

5.   Greenslade & Stuart 1984, p.97; and Massey, Donald 'History of Weston', www.westonstaffs.org.uk/details.php?pkid=86 (Accessed 9 July 2012)

6.   *A Topographical Dictionary of England* (1848), pp.668-672. URL: http://www. britishhistory.ac.uk/report.aspx?compid=50891. (Accessed 14 January 2013); Colwich Parish Council undated, p.8; and Bradley et al 1997, p.51.

7.   Conversation with Chris Larkin, granddaughter of Christopher and Ellen Sproston, 2 July 2012.

8.   Conversation with Chris Larkin, granddaughter of Christopher Sproston, 17 April 2013. Chris's comments on Christopher's narcolepsy corroborate much earlier family accounts provided by Christopher's daughter, Eleanor.

9.   Bradley et al 1997, p.18.

10. Phillips 1948, p.109; and Bradley et al 1997, p.18.

11. Phillips 1948, p.109; and Bradley et al 1997, p.18.

12. Bradley et al 1997, p.18.

13. Quoted in Brookes et al, 2008, p.8.

14. Bradley et al 1997, p.17.

15. Perkin 1970, p.58.

16. Wolmar 2008, p.1.

17. Court 1967, p.47.

18. Court 1967, pp.47, 166; and Perkin 1970, p.72.

19. Mathias 2001, p.253.

20. Wolmar 2008, pp.25-6.

21. BBC, 'Locomotion: Dan Snow's History of Railways' Episode 1, broadcast on BBC2, 15 January 2013; and Wolmar 2008, pp.39-40.

22. Perkin 1970, p.77.

23. Greenslade & Stuart 1984, p.97.

24. BBC, 'Locomotion: Dan Snow's History of Railways' Episode 2, broadcast on BBC2, 22 January 2013.

25. Greenslade & Stuart 1984, p.97.

26. Coleman 2000, p.20.

27. Perkin 1970, p.89; and Coleman 2000, p.26.

28. Coleman 2000, p.71.

29. BBC, 'Locomotion: Dan Snow's History of Railways' Episode 1, broadcast on BBC2, 15 January 2013.

30. Perkin 1970, pp.89-91.

31. Coleman 2000, Chapter 5.

32. Court 1967, p.170; and Coleman 2000, Chapter 8.

33. Perkin 1970, p.91; and Coleman 2000, pp.28, 121-2 & Chapter 5.

34. Reported in Mathias 2001, p.287.

35. May 1996, pp.185, 197; BBC, 'Locomotion: Dan Snow's History of Railways' Episode 2, broadcast on BBC2, 22 January 2013; and Greenslade & Stuart 1984, p.97.

36. May 1996, p.185.

37. May 1996, p.178; and Perkin 1970, pp.92, 99-100.

38. Perkin 1970, p.92.

39. BBC, 'Locomotion: Dan Snow's History of Railways' Episode 1, broadcast on BBC2, 15 January 2013.

40. Wolmar 2008, pp.41-2.

41. 'Economic infrastructure and institutions: Roads and transport', A History of the County of Cheshire: Volume 5 part 2: The City of Chester: Culture, Buildings, Institutions, 2005, pp.73-83. URL: www.british-history.ac.uk/report.aspx?compid=57309 (Accessed: 19 June 2012); Greenslade & Stuart 1984, p.99; May 1996, p.175; and Bagwell & Mingay 1970, p.31.

42. Brown 2010, pp.75-6; and Wolmar 2008, pp.119-20.

43. Bagwell & Mingay 1970, p.31; and May 1996, p.180.

44. Bagwell & Mingay 1970, p.32; and Wilkes 2011, p.17.

45. Perkin 1970, p.114.

46. Wolmar 2008, pp.60-1.

47. May 1996, p.177.

48. May 1996, p.177.

49. BBC, 'Locomotion: Dan Snow's History of Railways' Episode 2, broadcast on BBC2, 22 January 2013.

50. Manning, Sanchez, 'Slave-owners given huge payouts after abolition', The Independent on Sunday, 24 February 2013; and 'Legacies of British Slave-ownership', University College London. www.ucl.ac.uk/lbs. (Accessed 3 March 2013)

51. Manning, Sanchez, 'Slave-owners given huge payouts after abolition', The Independent on Sunday, 24 February 2013.

52. Harrington, Ralph, in 'A Revolution in Five Acts: 1 The Railways', presented by Ian Hislop, broadcast on Radio 4, January 2001.

53. Manning, Sanchez, 'Slave-owners given huge payouts after abolition', The Independent on Sunday, 24 February 2013.

54. Coleman 2000, p.39.

55. BBC, 'Locomotion: Dan Snow's History of Railways' Episode 2, broadcast on BBC2, 22 January 2013.

56. Wolmar, p.63.

57. BBC, 'Locomotion: Dan Snow's History of Railways' Episode 2, broadcast on BBC2, 22 January 2013.

58. 'Shugborough', www.staffordshire.gov.uk/leisure/museums/exhibitions/shug borough/Shugborough.aspx (Accessed 14 January 2013); and Stafford Record Office, Documents D615/EL/14, Agreements with the Trent Valley Railway Company for the construction of the line through Shugborough Park, 1845 & 1853.

59. 'Shugborough then and now: a brief history of the Shugborough Estate', www. shugborough.cmhosts.net/HistoryOfShugborough-138. (Accessed 19 June 2012)

60. 'Shugborough then and now: a brief history of the Shugborough Estate', www. shugborough.cmhosts.net/HistoryOfShugborough-138. (Accessed 19 June 2012)

61. Sproston 2007, p.59.

62. 'Shugborough', www.staffordshire.gov.uk/leisure/museums/exhibitions/shu gborough/Shugborough.aspx (Accessed 14 January 2013); Staffordshire County Council 1969; Staffordshire County Council 1974; and Baker, Andrew, 'Expanding the Estate', http://www.heardmusic.co.uk/Expanding_ the_Estate.html. (Accessed 9 April 2013)

63. Marx 1976, p.891.

64. Fairlie 2009.

65. Engels 1969, pp.286-95.

66. Bagwell & Mingay 1970, p.61; and Ashworth 1972, p.48.

67. Ashworth 1972, p.48.

68. Bagwell & Mingay 1970, pp.61-2.

69. Perkin 1970, p.55.

70. 'Shugborough then and now: a brief history of the Shugborough Estate', www. shugborough.cmhosts.net/HistoryOfShugborough-138. (Accessed 19 June 2012)

71. Bradley et al 1993, p.9.

72. Sproston 2007, p.63.

73. Sproston 2007, p.60.

74. Stafford Record Office, Document D615/EL/8/144/1909, 'Navigation Inn and Farm, Little Haywood' (part of the 'Records of the Anson Family of Shugborough, Earls of Lichfield' collection).

75. Bradley et al 1993, p.5.

76. BBC, 'Locomotion: Dan Snow's History of Railways' Episode 2, broadcast on BBC2, 22 January 2013.

77. Wolmar 2008, p.105.

78. BBC, 'Locomotion: Dan Snow's History of Railways' Episode 2, broadcast on BBC2, 22 January 2013.

79. Wolmar 2008, p.87.

80. Perkin 1970, pp.179-80.

81. Perkin 1970, p.180.

82. BBC, 'Locomotion: Dan Snow's History of Railways' Episode 2, broadcast on BBC2, 22 January 2013.

83. http://www.historyofyork.org.uk/themes/Victorian/the-railway-king-george-hudson. (Accessed 20 February 2013).

84. BBC, 'Locomotion: Dan Snow's History of Railways' Episode 2, broadcast on BBC2, 22 January 2013.

85. Wolmar 2008, pp.143-4.

86. Wolmar 2008, p.145.

87. Mathias 2001, pp.262-3.

88. Ashworth 1972, p.111.

89. BBC, 'Locomotion: Dan Snow's History of Railways' Episode 3, broadcast on BBC2, 29 January 2013.

90. May 1996, p.186.

91. Wolmar 2008, Chapter 9.

92. Wolmar 2008, pp.217-9.

93. Perkin 1970, pp.107, 112.

94. Department of Transport 1988.

95. May 1996, p.186.

96. Wolmar 2008, p.155.

97. Wolmar 2008, p.160; and Bagwell & Mingay 1970, p.30.

98. Wolmar 2008, pp.153-4, 221-2, 255; and Wojtczak 2005, p.117.

99. May 1996, p.183.

100. Bagwell & Mingay 1970, pp.30-31.

101. Wolmar 2008, pp.155-6.

102. Wolmar 2008, pp.202-3.

103. Wolmar 2008, pp.207-8.

104. May 1996, p.174.

105. BBC, 'Navigation Farm, Lt. Haywood', Domesday Reloaded, 1986. http://www.bbc.co.uk/history/domesday/dblock/GB-400000-321000/page/6. (Accessed 20 May 2013)

106. Kelly's Directories of Staffordshire, 1904 & 1908.

107. Kelly's Trade Directory of Staffordshire, 1912.

108. 1911 England Census record for James Sproston.

109. Kelly's Trade Directory of Staffordshire, 1916; and England & Wales, National Probate Calendar (Index of Wills & Administration), 1858-1966.

110. Kelly's Trade Directory of Staffordshire, 1916.

Chapter 7

1. Court 1967, p.166.

2. Perkin 1970, pp.277-8 & 282-3; and BBC, 'Locomotion: Dan Snow's History of Railways' Episode 3, broadcast on BBC2, 29 January 2013.

3. Extracts from article in *The Times*, reproduced in Court 1965, pp.208-10.

4. Perkin 1970, pp.283-4.

5. Bagwell & Mingay 1970, pp.32-3.

6. Mathias 2001, pp.257-60.

7. Wolmar 2008, pp.xiii, 67, 109.

8. Perkin 1970, pp.172, 176.

9. Mathias 2001, p.256.

10. Pearson 1977, pp.265-6.

11. May 1996, p.184; and Wolmar 2008, pp.83-4.

12. 'Final Report from Her Majesty's Commissioners on Agriculture, 1882', C. 3309, vol. XIV, in Court 1965, pp.38-43 ; and Bagwell & Mingay 1970, p.34.

13. Bagwell & Mingay 1970, p.34.

14. Bagwell & Mingay 1970, p.234.

15. Perkin 1970, pp.194-5.

16. Perkin 1970, p.115.

17. Court 1967, p.169.

18. Wolmar 2008, p.143.

19. Wolmar 2008, p.131.

20. Wolmar 2008, p.131.

21. Perkin 1970, p.42.

22. Bradley et al 1997, p.51.

23. Perkin 1970, p.170.

24. Wolmar 2008, pp.104-5.

25. Wolmar 2008, p.84.

26. Wolmar 2008, pp.117, 118, 326; and BBC, 'Locomotion: Dan Snow's History of Railways' Episode 2, broadcast on BBC2, 22 January 2013.

27. May 1996, p.184; and Wolmar 2008, p.73.

28. Perkin 1970, pp.118-9, 123-4, 238.

29. May 1996, p.185.

30. Rex, J A, 'The Sociology of a Zone of Transition' in Pahl 1968, pp.211-231; and Perkin 1970, pp.133-4.

31. Perkin 1970, pp.239-40.

32. Paraphrased from Perkin 1970, pp.243-4.

33. Perkin 1970, p.243.

34. Perkin 1970, pp.169 & 269-70.

35. Bagwell & Mingay 1970, pp.29-30; Court 1967, p.165; and May 1996, p.179.

36. Perkin 1970, pp.116-7.

37. BBC, 'Locomotion: Dan Snow's History of Railways' Episode 2, broadcast on BBC2, 22 January 2013; and Perkin 1970, pp.226-32.

38. Perkin 1970, p.218.

39. Wolmar 2008, p.142.

40. Wolmar 2008, p.268.

41. Wolmar 2008, p.114.

42. May 1996, p.355; Marwick 1971, p.12; and BBC, 'Locomotion: Dan Snow's History of Railways' Episode 3, broadcast on BBC2, 29 January 2013.

43. Wolmar 2008, p.228.

44. Wolmar 2008, p.252.

45. 'Railway Stations Around Cannock Chase', http://www.cannockchasehistory. org.uk/_Railways.htm.

46. 'Shugborough', p.12, www.staffordshire.gov.uk/leisure/museums/exhibitions/ shugborough/Shugborough.aspx. (Accessed 14 January 2013)

47. Colwich Parish Council undated, p.9. See also Staffordshire County Council 1969.

48. Bradley et al 1997, pp.6, 65, 100.

49. Bradley et al 1997, p.69; and http://www.palmer.staffscc.net/content/ employment. (Accessed 1 August 2013)

50. Quoted in Colwich Parish Council undated, p.11.

51. Colwich Parish Council undated, p.11.

52. Staffordshire County Council 1969.

53. BBC, Domesday Reloaded, 'The Ring at Little Haywood', 1986, http:// www.bbc.co.uk/history/domesday/dblock/GB-400000-321000/paGE/11. (Accessed 20 May 2013); and Bradley et al 1997, p.77.

54. Staffordshire County Council 1974.

55. http://www.britishlistedbuildings.co.uk/en-445180-school-house-and-old-school-building-att. (Accessed 21 May 2013)

56. Wilkes 2011, pp.62, 90-91.

57. UK census 1851, 1861.

58. Staffordshire County Council 1974; www.staffspasttrack.org.uk; BBC, 'Domesday Reloaded: Colwich School', 1986 http://www.bbc.co.uk/history/domesday/dblock/GB-400000-321000/page/17. (Accessed 20 May 2013); Bradley et al 1997, p.35; and http://www.visitoruk.com/Stafford/colwich- great-haywood-and-little-haywood-C592-... (Accessed 20 May 2013)

59. Trubshaw 1876, p.14; and 'Colwich, Great Haywood & Little Haywood', http://visitoruk.com/Stafford/colwich-great-haywood-and-little-haywood-C592-... (Accessed 20 May 2013)

60. Sister Benedict Rowell, 'Baker's Continuing Influence on Benedictine Nuns', Paper given at a conference in Abergavenny, May 2000. http://www.colwichabbey.org.uk/people/influence.htm. (Accessed 21 May 2013); and http://www.cannockchasehistory.org.uk/places/greathaywood.htm. (Accessed 21 May 2013)

61. http://www.colwichabbey.org.uk.

62. Davies Giddy, MP, cited in Parris & Mason 1997, p.177 and Taylor et al 1995, p.274.

63. Sutherland 1971, p.27.

64. Robert Lowe, Primary and Classical Education, 1867, quoted in Taylor et al 1995, p.274.

65. Hansard, House of Commons Debate, 17 February 1870, col. 465.

66. Department of Education & Science 1970.

67. Murphy 1972, p.77.

68. Sutherland 1971, p.31.

69. Lester Smith 1965, p.193.

70. Earl Fortesque, 1880, quoted in Parris & Mason 1997, p.179.

71. Musgrave 2007, p.45.

72. Landes 2003, pp.341-2.

73. Richard Tangye, quoted in Waterhouse 1957, p.72.

74. Quoted in Lowndes 1937, p.19.

75. Bradley et al 1997, p.36.

76. Bradley et al 1997, p.36.

77. Staffordshire County Council, 'Raising of the School Leaving Age', https://education.staffordshire.gov.uk/NR/rdonlyres/ED650F9C-627F-4687-9048-AB783299E493/169842/2Historyofraisingofschoolleavingage2013.doc. (Accessed 14 May 2013)

78. Mingay 1990, p.86.

79. Murphy 1972, p.10.

80. *The Times*, 18 February 1870.

81. McCann 1969, p.20.

82. McCann 1969, p.21.

83. Ashby 1961, pp.16-21.

84. Leeds School Board poster, 1871 in Department of Education & Science 1970.

85. Bradford School Board Examination Paper, 19 October 1901 in Department of Education & Science 1970.

86. Cole 2004, p.526.

87. Sutherland 1971, p.45.

88. Bagwell & Mingay 1970, p.226.

89. H G Wells, Experiment in Autobiography, cited by Lowndes 1937, p.5.

90. McCann 1969, p.25.

91. BBC, 'Locomotion: Dan Snow's History of Railways' Episode 3, broadcast on BBC2, 29 January 2013.

92. BBC, 'Locomotion: Dan Snow's History of Railways' Episode 3, broadcast on BBC2, 29 January 2013.

93. Wolmar 2008, p.313.

94. Wolmar 2008, p.67.

95. http://www.nndb.com/people/906/000068702. (Accessed 2 September 2013)

Chapter 8

1. Marwick 1971, p.1.

2. Marwick 1971, p.1.

3. Four series of Lark Rise to Candleford were broadcast by the BBC between 2008 and 2011.

4. Conversation with Chris Larkin, granddaughter of Christopher Sproston, 17 April 2013.

5. Conversation with Chris Larkin, 17 April 2013.

6. Bradley et al 1997, p.96.

7. Conversation with Chris Larkin, 17 April 2013.

8. Sproston 2007, pp.60, 64.

9. Thompson 1979.

10. Conversation with Chris Larkin, 17 April 2013.

11. May 1996, p.355.

12. BBC, 'Locomotion: Dan Snow's History of Railways' Episode 3, broadcast on BBC2, 29 January 2013.

13. www.the-narrowboat.co.uk/Articles/. (Accessed 8 October 2012)

14. Retold by Hazel's daughter.

15. The Gallipoli reference is from Hazel's daughter. Sixty percent of the service records from the First World War were destroyed as a result of enemy bombing of the War Office in 1940, during the Second World War. Those for all four Sprostons who enlisted are missing although limited information can be gleaned from First World War medal cards and (in the case of Jack) from other sources.

16. British Army WW1 Medal Rolls Index Cards, 1914-1920 record for Christopher H Sproston; and http://1914-1918.net. (Accessed 25 June 2013)

17. 1911 Census.

18. This account was told by Albert's sister, Nel.

19. Sources: various family members, including Albert's sister Nel, his niece Joan and, much later, his niece, Chris Larkin (17 April 2013).

20. Conversation with Chris Larkin, 17 April 2013.

21. Conversation with Chris Larkin, 17 April 2013; and phone conversation with Chris Larkin 22 July 2013.

22. 'The Spanish Flu pandemic of 1918', http://www.historic-uk.com/HistoryUK/HistoryofBritain/The-Spanish-Flu-pandemic-... (Accessed 2 July 2013)

23. The details of Jack's death and the circumstances surrounding it can be found in the letter from Jack's Commanding Officer dated 30 October 1918 and official letter sent to Christopher Sproston from the Infantry Record Office dated 5 November 1918 (both of which can be accessed via the first-rate website on the 25th County of London Cyclist Battalion The London Regiment, compiled by Simon Parker-Galbreath – see http://www.25thlondon.com/jcs.htm) – and from two editions of the battalion magazine *The Londoner* (Vol. III, No.1, August-September1918, p.35; and Vol. III, No. 2, February 1919, p.53) which can also be accessed via the homepage of the website.

24. 1911 Census.

25. www.25thlondon.com/numbers.htm. (Accessed 28 October 2012)

26. Fitzpatrick 2011, p.113.

27. *The Londoner* Vol. III, No.2, p.53.

28. *The Londoner* Vol. III, No.2, p.53.

29. 25th County of London Cyclist Battalion The London Regiment, 'Regiment History', www.25thlondon.com/history.htm. (Accessed 28 October 2012)

30. Ahmed & Atkins 2013.

31. Ahmed & Atkins 2013.

32. 'Guardians of the Frontier', www.khyberpakthunkhwa.gov.pk (Accessed 3 July 2013); and Tim Moreman, 'The Development of Frontier Warfare 1914-1939', http://www.king-emperor.com?Articles-Frontier-Warfare-a3.htm. (Accessed 3 July 2013)

33. 25th County of London Cyclist Battalion The London Regiment, 'Regiment History', www.25thlondon.com/history.htm. (Accessed 28 October 2012)

34. See, for example, 'Waziristan Campaign 1917', http://www.25thlondon.com/waziristan.htm (extracts from The London Cycle Battalion).

35. Extract from *The London Cyclist Battalion*, 'a chronicle of events connected with the 25th County of London Cyclist Battalion…', published for the 25th London (Cyclist) Old Comrades Association, 1932, http://www.25thlondon.com/waziristan.htm. (Accessed 3 July 2013)

36. 'Waziristan Campaign 1917: From My Point of View', Diary of Private H Parker, 2 Platoon, A Company, 1/25th London Regiment. http://www.25thlondon.com/diary1.htm. (Accessed 3 July 2013)

37. 25th County of London Cyclist Battalion The London Regiment, 'Regiment History', www.25thlondon.com/history.htm. (Accessed 28 October 2012)

38. 25th County of London Cyclist Battalion The London Regiment, 'Amritsar Uprising 1919', www.25thlondon.com/amritsar.htm. (Accessed 8 July 2013)

39. Commonwealth War Graves Commission, http://yard.ccta.gov.uk/cwgc/register.nst/wwwcreateservicedetails?openagent&1437871. (Accessed 12 November 2000)

40. Commonwealth War Graves Commission, http://yard.ccta.gov.uk/cwgc/register.nst/wwwcreateservicedetails?openagent&1437871. (Accessed 12 November 2000)

41. British Army WW1 Medal Roll Index Card for William James Sproston, http://discovery.nationalarchives.gov.uk/SearchUI/Details?uri=D5340168. (Accessed 4 February 2014)

42. Various members of the Sproston clan have related the owl stories over the years, including Bernard's sister Nel.

43. Office for National Statistics, '170 Years of Industrial Change Across England and Wales', 5 June 2013, http://www.ons/rel/census-analysis/170-years-of-industry/170-years-of-industrial-changeponent.html. (Accessed 22 July 2013)

44. Conversations with family member 17 April 2013 and 22 July 2013.

45. Colwich Parish Council undated, p.7.

Bibliography

Ahmed, Akbar & Akins, Harrison, *Waziristan: 'The most dangerous place in the world'*, Al Jazeera English, 12 April, 2013. (http://www.aljazeera.com/indepth/opinion/2013/04/20134983149771365.html. Accessed 2 July 2013)

Albert, William, *TheTurnpike Road System in England: 1663-1840*, Cambridge University Press, 2006.

Allison, K J (ed) 'Hull, 1700-1835', *A History of the County of York East Riding: Volume 1: The City of Kingston-upon-Hull*, Open University Press, 1969, pp.174-214.

Ashby, M K, *Joseph Ashby of Tysoe 1859-1919*, Cambridge University Press, 1961.

Ashworth, William, *An Economic History of England 1870-1939*, Methuen, 1972.

Atkins, P J, 'Milk consumption and tuberculosis in Britain, 1850-1950', 1999, in Fenton, 2000, pp.83-95.

Bentley, R, Dobson, A, Grant, M & Roberts, D, *British Politics in Focus (2nd edition)*, Causeway Press, 1999.

Bagwell, Philip S & Mingay, G E, *Britain and America 1850-1939: a study of economic change*, Routledge & Kegan Paul, 1970.

Bradley, M, Maingay, J, Maingay, R, Mallett, G, Mallett, M, Moreton, M, Morris, P, *A True and Perfect Inventory....: A glimpse of life in the Haywoods in the 17th century from wills of that period*, Haywood Society, 1993.

Bradley M, Maingay, J, Mallett, G, Mallett, M, Moreton, M, Milne, B, Milne, I & Morris, P, *A Hearsay History of the Haywoods and Colwich 1900-1939*, Haywood Society, 1997.

Breach, R W & Hartwell, R M, *British Economy and Society 1870-1970*, Oxford University Press, 1972.

Briggs, Jeanette, *The Trent and Mersey Canal from the River Trent in Nottingham to the River Mersey at Preston Brook*, The River Thames Guide, undated.

Bristow, Joy, *The Local Historian's Glossary of Words and Terms*, Countryside Books, 2001.

Broadbridge, S R & E, 'Communication with Canals in the Stafford Area', *Staffordshire Industrial Archaeology Society Journal, Vol 1*, 1970, pp.8-27.

Brookes, P, Emberton, P, Jarrett, L, Lloyd, H, Maingay, J, Tyrie, M & Tyrie, S,

A Hearsay History Part II: The Haywoods and Colwich 1939-1945, Haywood Society, 2008.

Brown, Pete, *Man Walks Into a Pub: A Sociable History of Beer*, Pan Books (2nd edition), 2010.

Bryson, Bill, *At home: A Short History of Private Life*, Black Swan, 2011.

Bryson, Bill, *Shakespeare: The World as a Stage*, Harper Press, 2009.

Carlyle, Thomas, *Past and Present*, New York University Press, 1977 (originally published 1843).

Cole, M, '"Rule Britannia" and the New American Empire', *Policy Futures in Education, Vol. 2, Nos 3 & 4*, pp.523-538, 2004.

Coleman, Terry, *The Railway Navvies: A history of the men who made the railways*, Pimlico, 2000.

Colwich Parish Council, *Village Design Statement for the Parish of Colwich*, www.staffordbc.gov.uk, undated.

Court, W H B, *A Concise Economic History of Britain From 1750 to Recent Times*, Cambridge University Press, 1967.

Court, W H B, *British Economic History 1870-1914: Commentary and Documents*, Cambridge University Press, 1965.

Department of Education & Science, *Education Act 1870* (collection of documents), HMSO, 1970.

Department of Transport, *Railway Accident: Report on the Collision that occurred on 19th September 1986 at Colwich Junction*, HMSO, 1988.

Dobb, Maurice, 'Transition from Feudalism to Capitalism', *Our History No.29*, 1963.

Engels, Frederick, *The Condition of the Working Class in England*, Panther, 1969.

Engels, Friedrich, 'The Decline of Feudalism and the Rise of the Bourgeoisie', *Monthly Review,* April 1957, pp.445-454.

Evans, Richard J, *The Victorians: Life and Death*, Lecture given at the Museum of London, 13 December 2010 (www.gresham.ac.uk. Accessed 11 June 2012).

Fairlie, Simon, 'A Short History of Enclosure in Britain', *The Land, Issue 7*, Summer 2009.

Fenton, A, *Order and Disorder: the Health Implications of Eating and Drinking in the Nineteenth and Twentieth Centuries*, Tuckswell Press, 2000.

Fitzpatrick, Jim, *The Bicycle in Wartime: An Illustrated History*, Star Hill Studio, 2011.

Flinn, M W, 'The Poor Employment Act of 1817', *The Economic History Review, New Series: Vol 14, No 1*, 1961, pp.82-92.

Fort, Tom, *Downstream: Across England in a Punt*, Arrow, 2009.

Freer, Wendy, *Canal boat people, 1840-1997*, PhD thesis, University of Nottingham, 1991.

Greenslade, M W (ed), 'Lichfield: Domestic buildings and communications', *A History of the County of Stafford: Volume 14*, 1990.

Greenslade, M W & Stuart D G, *A History of Staffordshire*, Phillimore, 1984.

Hanson, Harry, *The Canal Boatmen 1760-1914*, Manchester University Press, 1975.

Haughton, Jonathan & Khandker, Shahidur, R, *Handbook on Poverty and Inequality*, World Bank, 2009.

Hobsbawm, E J, *Industry and Empire*, Penguin, 1999.

Hobsbawm, E J, *Labouring Men: Studies in the History of Labour*, Widenfeld & Nicolson, 1968.

Hobsbawm, E J, *The Age of Revolution 1789-1848,* Mentor, 1962.

Kelly's Directory of Staffordshire, 1896.

Kelly's Directory of Staffordshire, 1900.

Landes, David S, *The Unbound Prometheus: Technological Change and Industrial Development in Western Europe from 1750 to the Present*, Cambridge University Press, 2003.

Lead, Peter, *The Trent & Mersey Canal*, Moorland, 1980.

Lee, William, *Report to the General Board of Health on a preliminary inquiry into the sewerage, drainage and supply of water, and the sanitary conditions of the inhabitants of the Parish of Dudley in the county of Worcester*, London, 1852.

Lester Smith, W O, *Education: An Introductory Survey*, Penguin, 1965.

Lindsay, Jean, *The Trent and Mersey Canal*, David & Charles, 1979.

Lowndes, G A N, *The Silent Social Revolution: an Account of the Expansion of Public Education in England and Wales, 1895-1935*, 1937.

Light, Roy & Heenan, Susan, *Controlling Supply: The Concept of 'Need' in Liquor Licensing*, Bristol Centre for Criminal Justice, University of the West of England, 1999.

McCann, W P, 'Elementary Education in England and Wales on the Eve of the 1870 Education Act', *Journal of Educational Administration and History, Vol. II, No. 1*, pp.20-29, December 1969.

Mathias, Peter, *The First Industrial Nation: An Economic History of Britain 1700-1914*, Routledge, 2001.

Marwick, Arthur, *The Explosion of British Society, 1914-1970*, MacMillan, 1971.

Marx, Karl, *Capital Volume 1*, Penguin, 1976.

Marx, Karl, *The Class Struggles in France, 1848-1850*, International Publishers, 1964.

Marx, Karl & Engels, Frederick, *Selected Works in One Volume*, Lawrence & Wishart, 1968.

Matthews, Stanley, *The Way It Was: My Autobiography*, Headline, 2000.

May, Trevor, *An Economic and Social History of Britain 1760-1990,* Longman, 1996.

Merrill, John N, *Canal Walks Vol.3: Short Circular Walks of the Canals of Staffordshire*, JNM Publications, 1989.

Mingay, G E, *Rural Life in Victorian England*, Alan Sutton, 1990.

Morris, John, *Domesday Book: Staffordshire (24)*, Phillimore, 1976.

Murphy, J, *The Education Act 1870*, David & Charles, 1972.

Musgrave, P W, *Society and Education in England since 1800*, Routledge, 2007.

O'Farrell, John, *An Utterly Impartial History of Britain (or 2000 Years of Upper Class Idiots in Charge)*, Black Swan, 2008.

O'Riordan, Christopher, 'Civil War Squatters in the Middlewich House of Corection', *Cheshire History*, No. 18 (Autumn 1986), pp.21-3, Cheshire Local History Association, 1986.

Pahl, R E (ed), *Readings in Urban Sociology*, Pergamon Press, 1968.

Parris, Matthew & Mason, Phil, *Read My Lips: A Treasury of the Things Politicians Wish They Had Never Said*, Penguin, 1997.

Pearson, Hesketh, *The Smith of Smiths: Being the life, wit and humour of Sydney Smith*, Folio Society, 1977.

Pennant, Thomas, *The Journey from Chester to London*, unknown publisher, 1811.

Perkin, Harold, *The Age of the Railway*, Panther,1970.

Phillips, John F, *The Agricultural Act 1947*, Eyre & Spotiswode, 1948.

Pugh, Martin, *Women's Suffrage in Britain 1867-1928*, The Historical Association, 1980.

Pugh, Martin, 'Votes for Women', *Modern History Review*, September 1990, pp.30-31.

Raeburn, Antonia, *Militant Suffragettes*, New English Library, 1974.

Reay, Barry, 'The context and meaning of popular literacy: some evidence from nineteenth century rural England', *Past and Present*, No. 131 (May 1991) pp.89-129, Oxford University Press, 1991.

Rightmove plc, *The Rightmove Happy at Home Index*, February 2012.

Roberts, D R, *Ownership, Control and Management in the Class Structure*, unpublished MPhil thesis, University of Bradford, 1982.

Rover, Constance, *Women's Suffrage and Party Politics in Britain 1866-1914*, Routledge & Kegan Paul,1967.

Rowbotham, Sheila, *Hidden from History*, Pluto, 1973.

Saul, S B, *The Myth of the Great Depression 1873-1896*, MacMillan, 1969.

Sproston, Colin, *Noble Curios and Connections*, Trafford Publishing, 2007.

Stafford Borough Council Local Development Framework, *Revised Settlement Assessment of Services and Facilities*, June 2012.

Staffordia, *Supplement to the History of Haywood (with corrections)*, Allison & Bowen, 1930.

Staffordshire County Council, *Conservation Area 7: Great Haywood & Shugborough*, County Planning & Development Department Publication, November, 1969.

Staffordshire County Council, *Conservation Area 57: Colwich and Little Haywood*, County Planning & Development Department Publication, February, 1974.

Steel, Mark, *Vive La Revolution*, Scribner, 2004.

Sutherland, Gillian, *Elementary Education in the Nineteenth Century*, The Historical Association, 1971.

Taylor, P, Richardson, J, Yeo, A, Marsh, I, Trobe, K & Pilkington, A, *Sociology in Focus*, Causeway Press, 1995.

Thompson, E P, *The Making of the English Working Class*, Penguin, 1968.

Thompson, E P, 'Time, work, discipline and industrial capitalism', *Past and Present*, Vol.38 No.1, 1967, pp.56-97.

Thompson, Flora, *Lark Rise to Candleford*, Oxford University Press, 1979.

Townsend, Peter, *Poverty in the United Kingdom: A survey of household resources and stadards of living*, Penguin, 1979.

Trubshaw, Susanna, *Family Records*, R & W Wright [printers], Stafford, 1876. [Trubshaw family records book]

University of Portsmouth and others, A Vision of Britain Through Time, 2009. Available at www.visionofbritain.org.uk/

Waterhouse, Rachel E, *A Hundred Years of Engineering Craftsmanship: A Short History of Tangyes Ltd*, Tangyes Ltd, 1957.

Weber, Max, *The Protestant Ethic and the Spirit of Capitalism*, Unwin University Books, 1930.

Welch, C M, 'Glass-making in Wolseley, Staffordshire', *Post-Medieval Archaeology 31*, 1997, pp. 1-60.

White, William, *History, Gazetteer, and Directory of Staffordshire and the City and County of the City of Lichfield*, published by the author, 1834.

White, William, *History, Gazetteer, and Directory of Staffordshire and the City and County of the City of Lichfield*, published by the author, 1851.

Wilkes, Sue, *Tracing Your Canal Ancestors: A Guide for Family Historians*, Pen & Sword, 2011.

Wolmar, Christian, *Fire and Steam: How the Railways Transformed Britain*, Atlantic Books, 2008.

Wojtczak, Helena, *Railwaywomen: Exploitation, Betrayal and Triumph in the Workplace*, Hastings Press, 2005.

Youngson, A J, *Britain's Economic Growth 1920-1966*, Allen & Unwin, 1968.

Acknowledgements

Despite the undoubted benefits to the historian of online research, visits to libraries, archives and other public institutions are not only still essential but also hugely enjoyable. You meet people who still care about public service and who share your enthusiasm for discovery (but who know a lot more about how to achieve it). And it gets you out of the house. I am indebted therefore to staff at a number of these organisations and in particular to those at the county record office and the William Salt Library in Stafford, the delightful Shugborough-based members of the Staffordshire Archives and Heritage Service who look after the county museum collections, the helpful staff at the University of East Anglia Library, and to those performing valuable tasks at the National Archives at Kew.

Similarly, there is no proper substitute for leaving your desk to go walkabout. Much can be discovered about a village and its history from informed walks. Colwich Parish Council has published a folder of walks in and around the villages which I have put to good use. It is available from the friendly and welcoming tardis-like office at the Parish Centre in Little Haywood.

Jane Maingay and the Haywood Society deserve a special mention for their work in sustaining interest in the history of the villages of Colwich and Little and Great Haywood. In a number of places I have drawn on the three volumes produced by the society between 1993 and 2008; together they provide fascinating glimpses into the local history compiled from oral accounts of surviving residents as well as historical documents and photographs.

The memories, the knowledge and the personal family histories of close and wider members of the Sproston family have proved invaluable. I am especially grateful to Christine Larkin and Colin Sproston and to Susan Bradley, organiser of the Sproston Family History website.

Thanks are due to Simon Parker-Galbreath, compiler and manager of the excellent website of the 25th London (Cyclist)

Regiment, not least for assistance in making sense of the First World War military records of Jack Sproston's battalion. I have benefited, too, from the generous advice of Stafford author John Connor and his willingness to share his own publishing experiences. I should also thank the two Alans, John, Richard and Rob (collectively the Rivergarden 'chums') for always pleasant and not infrequently stimulating conversation over beers, coffee or lunch.

Finally, my thanks and appreciation go to Sally for her advice and active encouragement, to Ben for his consideration and thoughtfulness and to Anne who – in addition to providing all sorts of time-consuming technical help – somehow manages to combine honest criticism with enduring support.

Responsibility for any errors is, of course, mine. Every effort has been made to trace and acknowledge copyright holders for images appearing in this book but any information about omissions is welcomed. Photographs not specifically credited are from my personal collection.

An adapted version of the passage in the final chapter referring to Jack Sproston's First World War experiences has appeared in a different form in an article I wrote for Family Tree magazine.